HERE COMES JOY

Here Comes Joy
One Woman's Journey from Trauma to Transformation

Copyright © 2025 Sandi Ellis

All rights reserved. No part of this publication may be reproduced in a retrieval system, or transmitted in any form or by any means—electronic, mechanical, photocopying, recording, or otherwise—without the prior written permission of the publisher.

Scriptures taken from the Holy Bible, New International Version®, NIV®. Copyright © 1973, 1978, 1984, 2011 by Biblica, Inc.™ Used by permission of Zondervan. All rights reserved worldwide. www.zondervan.com The "NIV" and "New International Version" are trademarks registered in the United States Patent and Trademark Office by Biblica, Inc.™ | Scripture quotations marked (NLT) are taken from the Holy Bible, New Living Translation, copyright ©1996, 2004, 2015 by Tyndale House Foundation. Used by permission of Tyndale House Publishers, Carol Stream, Illinois 60188. All rights reserved. | Scripture taken from the New King James Version®. Copyright © 1982 by Thomas Nelson. Used by permission. All rights reserved.

While precaution has been taken in the preparation of this book, the publisher and author assume no responsibility for errors or omissions, or for damages resulting from the use of the information contained herein. This is a work of nonfiction. Some names, identifying characteristics, places, events, and timelines have been changed or adjusted to protect the privacy of individuals and to preserve narrative flow. Any resemblance to actual persons, living or dead, or actual events is not intended to be misleading or defamatory.

This book is set in the typeface *Athelas* designed by Veronika Burian and Jose Scaglione.

Paperback ISBN: 978-1-967262-15-1
Hardcover ISBN: 979-8-8693-1264-8

A Publication of *Tall Pine Books*
PO Box 42 Warsaw | Indiana 46581
www.tallpinebooks.com

| 1 25 25 20 16 02 |

Published in the United States of America

**ONE WOMAN'S JOURNEY
FROM TRAUMA *to* TRANSFORMATION**

HERE COMES
Joy

SANDI ELLIS

To Jesus Christ, my Lord and Savior. You are my greatest Treasure and the source of every good thing in my life. I pray that the revelation of Your heart for us will flow through every page of this book. May You meet each reader right where they are—whole or broken, joyful or sorrowful—and draw them closer to You.

Endorsements

I met Sandi in Chapter 8 of this book, and she always radiated joy from the moment I met her! Truly, I would never have imagined the details she experienced, as described in the first seven chapters. As you read through the pages of *Here Comes Joy*, may you come to discover—just as Sandi has—that it is not our own strength that carries us through life's trials, but the joy found in the loving presence of Jesus. For in His presence there is fullness of joy, and His joy is our strength. May these truths, along with Sandi's powerful testimony, point you to Jesus—the Source of joy. His joy will propel you forward, knowing *you* were the joy set before Him when He endured the cross.

CHRISTINE VALES

His Appointed Times and *Christine Vales Ministries*

Here Comes Joy is more than a memoir—it's a prophetic roadmap of redemption, healing, and God's relentless pursuit of His children. Sandi Ellis writes with raw honesty and deep spiritual insight, inviting readers into her journey from pain to purpose, from abandonment to identity, and ultimately, from survival to supernatural joy.

With each chapter, you witness the beauty of a life fully surrendered to Christ. Sandi's story is proof that God still heals, still speaks through dreams, and still writes the most unexpected love stories. Her voice is both tender and bold—grounded in Scripture, forged through suffering, and overflowing with wisdom.

Stacye and I are honored to stand with Sandi as she releases this life-giving work. *Here Comes Joy* will not just move you—it will transform you.

MICHAEL MCINTYRE
Entrepreneur | Kingdom Coach |
Founder of *Next Level Experience*

In *Here Comes Joy*, Sandi Ellis offers more than a memoir—she extends a lifeline. Through raw honesty and Spirit-breathed wisdom, she reminds us that even in life's harshest soils, beauty can bloom. From the rough terrain of Los Angeles to the sacred spaces of ministry, her story is one of resilience, surrender, and the relentless pursuit of wholeness in Christ.

What makes this well-written book so moving isn't just Sandi's ability to recount tragedy and triumph—it's her unwavering testimony that God wastes nothing. Every scar becomes a story; every broken place, a birthplace for new life. Like the street flower she describes, Sandi shows us how to rise—not rooted in perfect circumstances, but in the perfect love of a redeeming God.

This book is for those in need of a breakthrough—for the wounded, the weary and anyone who cherish a story of redemption. It's a declaration that healing is possible, purpose is within reach, and joy truly comes in the morning.

As Psalm 30:5 beautifully promises,

"Weeping may endure for a night, but joy cometh in the morning."

Sandi's journey proves that morning always comes when we are rightly positioned in Christ.

CLINT DAY
Radio host and podcaster

How trauma can become holy ground. The world needs this book!

BILL YOUNT
Blowing the Shofar Ministries

What an amazing gift I've been given—to watch Sandi walk out from the wreckage of her past into the fulfillment of God's purposes and plans for her life. Sandi truly operates in the fullness of her identity in Christ! She powerfully, selflessly, and with compassion, she is able to join people in their pain—because of the healing she has experienced on her journey! Sandi is confident that God would love to step into the ruins of every person's life and rebuild it to be better than anything they could ever imagine. Time and time again, I've seen God use the devastation that Sandi experienced in her early life to provide help, hope, and healing to others who are suffering. Every page will point to the divine intervention that transformed her life—and will continually point to the One who is able to redeem every heartache that we encounter in this life. You won't want to miss this story of redemption!

DEBBY TEMMER, MA, LPC,
CEO, *Centered for Life*

"Here Comes Joy" is a life-transformational must-read! Sandi Ellis has tremendous insight and knowledge, with deep revelations on overcoming real-life traumatic experiences. The Holy Spirit utilizes Sandi to unveil rooted issues to bring deliverance and healing to the downcast and brokenhearted. She carries a yoke-breaking anointing and JOY with the love of Christ Jesus!

Sandi and her husband, Jarrett, are a loving and powerful couple who flow in the Holy Spirit as they minister together across America and internationally. Camille and I highly encourage you to read this book and invite them to your church or event!

STAN LOVINS II
Revival Evangelist,
Sandlot Ministries, Revivals for Jesus
www.Stanlovins.com

Contents

Foreword *1*

PART 1: PLANTED IN PAIN

1. Street Flower 7
2. Becoming Invisible 31
3. Think Again 47
4. Toxic Ownership 65

PART 2: PRUNED FOR PURPOSE

5. There's No Grid for Grief 83
6. Layers of Healing 101
7. A New Garment 119
8. Swapping Coasts 137

PART 3: PROPELLED INTO PROMISE

9. Platforms 155
10. Innerworkings 175
11. Dreams: Assembly Required 193
12. Now and Forever 223

Gallery *250*
Acknowledgements *255*
About the Author *257*

Foreword

Here Comes Joy is a masterpiece of healing the pain of your past into the hope and promise of your future. Many of us, when we have physical pain, go to the doctor for an MRI, but *Here Comes Joy* becomes a spiritual ultrasound—an MRI—targeting the secret sorrows of our lives. Prophetess Sandi has the God-given sensitivity to use laser-beam truth that provides deliverance and healing through Christ Jesus.

The first time I met Prophetess Sandi Ellis was on a Friday evening in one of our seminars. As I walked in, she was toward the back of the room. I will never forget that Sandi was in my heart from that moment forward. A few months later, when I was leaving service, Sandi handed me a letter. Upon reading the letter, I realized that Sandi was being used in an astronomical way to help the marginalized—those who have no hope and those who are destitute. The compassion given to her by the Holy Spirit reaches into the deepest depths of one's despair.

In the letter, she brought to my attention her deep concerns for a single mom with three children, who had been homeless and was in desperate need of a car. She had to take the bus to work at 3:30 a.m., leaving her children in the shelter because she had found a job. Sandi's concerns over her car impressed me so much, and through her kindness, we were able to obtain a car for that precious single mother. Such compassion is drawn from experiences that we go through in life, which can either make us cold, calloused, and angry—or can be used for the glory of God as a tool of sensitivity that liberates others from their personal pain. These are the spiritual emancipators, and Prophetess Sandi Ellis is one of them.

Sandi Ellis has a unique gift of incorporating the Scriptures and insight into our personal pain and trauma, bringing us to the hope and living reality of possessing the promises of God. *Here Comes Joy* will provide anyone, from any age or stage in life, with the spiritual and emotional tools for deliverance, deep inner healing, and the courage to pick up the pieces and start again.

Sandi uses her own traumatic emotional and psychological obstacles that—even as a child—presented themselves as insurmountable challenges that could have blocked her destiny for the rest of her life. However, *Here Comes Joy* becomes the living reality that it is possible to courageously confront the giants and turn them into opportunities that have led her to a place of obtaining what Paul describes in Ephesians 3:20 as "exceeding abundantly above all we could ask or think, according to the power that works in us." If you are experiencing the difficulty of severing the soul ties and emotional experiences that keep your destiny in a prison of pain; if you have been trying to escape the feeling of being pulled into a pit of despair; or if you are just seeking more refined character traits—*Here Comes Joy* will help you, step by step, to achieve those goals.

Sandi's Destiny Coaching provides scriptural techniques that help us in a practical manner to achieve Christlike character, which becomes the door of destiny in our lives. She uses examples of those in the Scriptures who were faced with insurmountable tests and trials that should have emotionally debilitated them—but instead, she shows us how to overcome such challenges through their examples. She shows us how to possess the promises of God.

By reading *Here Comes Joy*, expect a closer relationship with Christ—a lifelong companion in the form of a book.

Expect the Holy Spirit to bring a mantle of impartation and divine liberation for all your inner healing needs. *HCJ* will bring you into fellowship with the Holy Spirit and help you understand how God places a price tag on your pain and uses it for His glory.

Sincerely in Christ,

DR. MICHELLE CORRAL
Foundress of *Breath of the Spirit International Ministries*

PART 1
Planted in Pain

CHAPTER ONE
Street Flower

"Do not despise these small beginnings, for the Lord rejoices to see the work begin." (Zechariah 4:10)

Past the salty California coast, through sunbaked streets, beyond the Hollywood Hills and south of downtown Los Angeles, you will find a tightly packed, working-class neighborhood called South Gate. Here, kids walk the worn sidewalks to school, passing mural-covered concrete walls. Chain-link fences border small stucco homes—usually rented by the occupants. Inside those homes are families of all kinds—broken, blended, happy, dysfunctional, sad, beautiful *families*.

Some are chasing the American dream. Others didn't know there was a dream to chase to begin with. Most are surviving, and those who are thriving usually find a way out. It was a safe, all-American city in the 1960s, and even when I was born in June of 1973, it was a respectable community. By 1980, the Firestone plant and General Motors, and half a dozen other major factories shut down, leaving the South Gate economy in pieces. As the economy went down, crime went up. It was no longer the quaint, cozy neighborhood that many once knew, but a sketchy shell of what it used to be.

This was the soil I started in.

We all begin our lives planted in something. For some, it's a nutrient-rich environment, fed by the love of godly parents and the outstretched arms of a prosperous community. For others, the soil leaves much to be desired. To truly flourish in South Gate, you almost felt like a pavement plant—growing up through the cracks of the sidewalk, defying the odds, and blooming in a harsh setting. The kind of plants that push through city sidewalks aren't delicate roses or well-tended garden flowers. They're tough, strong, and stubbornly alive.

They don't get the luxury of careful watering or shade from the sun—but somehow, they find a way. Urban plants don't bloom because conditions are perfect. They bloom because it's in their nature to reach for the light—even when the opening is small. And maybe that's what it meant to grow up here: learning to push through, to stretch toward something greater, to find strength in struggle. Sometimes, the most beautiful things aren't the ones planted in perfect conditions, but the ones that rise where no one thought they could.

The truth is, I was born into a quickly changing world. Just five months before I came along, *Roe v. Wade* was decided, making abortion legal throughout America. My mother, despite her struggles, chose life—and for that, I am forever grateful, knowing the alternative would have been easy. She herself grew up in Lynwood, which sits between South Gate and Compton. Born in the middle of the 20th century, she was shaped by serious dysfunction in the household she was born into.

Her father—my grandpa George—was a World War II veteran who stormed the beaches of Normandy. After the war, ready to settle down, he married my grandmother, Mercy. They started their young lives together in Oregon before moving to California, where they had my mom and her brother.

George opened a mechanic shop and worked hard while Mercy took a clerical job. They had their hands full building a life and needed help with the children. As a result, they decided to hire a babysitter—which was fine until the day Mercy came home from work and found George in bed with her.

Utterly devastated, Mercy ran out of the house—*without* the children—and simply did not come back. For my mom, this was a defining moment. She had her life before this event, and her life after—and they were two very different realities. She was left behind with an unfaithful father who, hardened by war, did not have the emotional capacity to nurture her and her baby brother. It was a rigid, emotionally distant, survival-based upbringing.

As the years wore on, Mercy met a man named Ray and remarried, eventually returning to California to reclaim her children. By then, though, years of absence made for a cold welcome home. My mother was angry and, along with her brother, refused to go with their mother. Mercy did remain in contact with them, but the maternal bond was shattered, by no fault of the children. Thus, my mother was raised in a home without a mother's warmth.

In the same town, around the same time, my father, Bobby McGuire, was going through abandonment in his own unique way. His father—William McGuire, also known as Chief Wah-Nee-Ota—was a man of contradictions. He was a Creek Nation chief, a traveling musician, and a Hollywood actor, appearing alongside figures like Eleanor Roosevelt and advising on films like *Flaming Star* with Elvis Presley. He had charisma, talent, connections, and a name that carried weight.

But he also had secrets. The main one being a *second* family. Growing up, my father and his sister Nadine believed their family was just like any other. Sure, Dad would travel for work, but don't all dads? Their naïveté ended when they met a group of children at school with the same last name. The McGuire kids all looked at each other, all having similar features and the same name, and one asked, "Who's your dad?"

"William McGuire. Chief Wah-Nee-Ota."

My father's stomach must have dropped.

That's our dad, too.

That night, they ran home and told their mother, Judy, the news. Furious, she marched across town and found William at another woman's house—surrounded by half a dozen children that he had secretly sired. A second family, a double life. After being confronted with his massive web of deception, my grandfather made a choice. He left my father and Nadine behind and stayed with the other family from then on out.

From that moment on, my father grew up without a dad. And the mother he was left with was not the comforting, maternal type, to say the least. In truth, she was an alcoholic—and not the quiet, sad kind of alcoholic, but a raging one. She was a woman hardened by life, by abandonment, by wounds that had never healed. Verbal and physical abuse were the norm during her drunken tirades. I would say my father never truly recovered from it. Emotionally, he was stuck at age 10, frozen in an era of trauma.

As he grew up, he was relentlessly bullied in school. Even worse, after meeting my mom in high school, one of his tormenters was my mother's brother. The pattern of abuse seemed to follow him wherever he went. Nevertheless, my parents fell in love before they were old enough to buy a lottery ticket. They were two broken kids who probably thought they could make each other whole.

My dad was tall and handsome, with kind eyes and a dark complexion. Like my mother, he too had a playful, childlike sense of humor. They moved in together, fresh out of high school, and had me no more than a year later. At the time, a very small percentage of children were born out of wedlock, and I happened to be one. It was something

I had to heal from after many years—the feeling of *illegitimacy*. When you're born out of wedlock, it can write a subconscious message in your heart that says: *I wasn't supposed to be here*. That internal narrative can be incredibly damaging if it's left unchecked. Inner healing has allowed me to reframe that, which we will discover later in the book.

My parents wasted no time multiplying. My older brother Justin was almost a year old when I was born, Rachel showed up a year after me, and Margie came along two years after her. My dad worked blue-collar jobs while my mother stayed home with us, getting by on limited means, yet doing the best they could. My early memories are hazy, but I recall a feeling from the top down that "children should be seen and not heard," which meant I often stayed in the background of any scene. It's worth noting that I realize no one ever taught my parents how to be parents. There was no manual handed to them, no course on how to raise children with emotional safety and connection. They simply repeated what they knew—what had been modeled for them. Their parents were just trying to survive, fortunate if they could keep food on the table. So, it's no wonder that nurturing, emotional attunement, or gentle correction weren't part of the equation.

Understanding this gives me a healthy perspective. They were barely more than kids themselves, trying to raise four of their own straight out of high school. They did the best they could with the tools they had. And while their best sometimes fell short, I can now see the weight they were carrying. Hindsight brings compassion. While my dad labored from paycheck to paycheck, he did have a bright spot in his life: music. He could make a guitar speak. He played in bars, on worship teams, anywhere that would have him. He had stories about playing with *The Carpenters*, rubbing shoulders with musicians who had made it, though he never made it big himself.

He had talent without stability, a gift without direction.

He and I were close when I was little. I was the one who resembled him most. While my siblings had my mother's German-European features, Justin and I had his. In my innocence, I never registered his sense of abandonment, nor did I consider the possibility that he would perpetuate that painful cycle. I was just five years old when the news came down from my mom after multiple inquiries.

"Your dad has left, and he isn't coming back."

No explanation. No reasons were given, no goodbyes were exchanged. He just left. I wouldn't crawl into his lap anymore, and I would no longer hear his guitar in the other room. I wouldn't giggle at his jokes anymore. Age five should have been the wonderful start of building early, lasting memories with my dad. Instead, it became the funeral of my childhood.

I have a vivid memory of seeing him again very briefly, probably when he came to pick up a few of his things. I recall scowling at him, my small way of expressing the hurt and confusion I didn't know how to articulate. I failed to understand that he was not leaving me, but leaving my mom. As a child, you take it all personally, and I certainly did. It felt like he was abandoning me, not just physically but emotionally.

Children internalize everything. They see their parents as superheroes, so if something goes wrong, they assume it's their own fault. A child's logic says: if Superman avoids me, it's not because he is doing something wrong; it's because *I* am bad.

The split between my parents was difficult enough—but the silence that followed was its own kind of wound. When my dad left, it unknowingly planted a belief deep in my heart: that all men would always leave. Over time, that quiet lie began to weave itself through every relationship I had. What was once a single, painful event slowly became a lens through which I saw the world—shaping the way

I viewed love, trust, and especially the presence of significant men in my life.

Sometimes I wonder how much healing might have come from just a few simple words: "It's not your fault." Or perhaps someone gently telling me, "It's OK to feel sad or angry. Your feelings matter—you're allowed to express them." Words like those could have offered something solid to stand on—something larger than the pain that felt so overwhelming at the time. In the absence of that kind of reassurance, kids are left to make sense of things on their own—and too often, it's shame that fills in the silence.

What started as a fairly typical South Gate childhood gradually became something heavier, marked by the ache of abandonment passed down through generations. The soil I was planted in—already difficult—grew even tougher to take root in.

Looking back now, I can only imagine how scared and heartbroken my mother must have been—suddenly alone, with four children to raise. She was barely more than a child herself, just out of high school, doing her best to carry the weight of something so much bigger than she'd ever prepared for. This must have substantiated deeper abandonment wounds for my mom—validating fears that she may have carried long before my father ever left. And just like me, perhaps she, too, was left filling in the blanks, without anyone to remind her: "It's not your fault. You're allowed to feel. You're not alone."

* * *

"Hey, you guys OK? Where are you heading?"

"Oh, just walking to school," we'd say to the officers.

"Ok, just be safe. Here, take a couple baseball cards."

These types of interactions with local police were normal as we'd walk 6 blocks to Bryson Elementary, or later nearly two miles to the high school—rain or shine. Some kids were lucky enough to be dropped off, but my two feet were my vehicle for most of my childhood.

Confidence doesn't materialize out of thin air and just hit you one day—it's instilled by parents, leaders, teachers, or mentors. For me as a young child, with a young mother who was trying to survive with four children, I had yet to get that instillation. In school, I was shy and awkward, clinging to my mom's leg the first day of preschool, riddled with separation anxiety as the administrator physically pried me away from her.

Eventually, I settled into the routine, but by no means became an extrovert. I favored subjects like science and history, but would check out during the others. At home, television became an escape for me, a window into a world that felt safer and more comforting than my own. I loved watching *Little House on the Prairie* and *The Waltons*. If I had to retroactively analyze myself, I would say I was drawn to a picture of happy families, kind parents, warm homes with a strong father figure, and a sense of belonging. On the other hand, I also loved *The Twilight Zone* reruns. Just maybe I was comforted by seeing a reality that was even more backwards and wonky than my own.

When school was out for the year, we'd pass our summers in the community pool. South Gate offered yearly passes, and we would splash and play until our fingers pruned. We would run around the large park and rec center, causing trouble and making friends—or attending the occasional Dodgers game with the Lyn-Gate church group. Sometimes we would have a potluck at the beach, and the church would perform baptisms.

Even at a young age, I noticed I had a foot in two worlds. I had my standard neighborhood friends, and I had my church friends. Stephanie Flack lived in an apartment behind our house, and I would often walk across the alleyway to hang out with her. She was about a year older and incredibly worldly in my eyes. She didn't have the typical Christian household, and her family's perspective fascinated me. She introduced me to cable TV—something we initially lacked at home—and we'd spend hours watching MTV and Madonna music videos. Through her, I was being schooled in life outside the church bubble.

On the other hand, I had my church friends and church activities. Names like Cynthia Manous and Tommy Garcia come to mind. With Tommy, our moms were friends, and the families would get together for camping and outings now and then. Like my own, his family didn't have it all together, but he remained optimistic, funny, and loyal.

Cynthia lived near the church, where my family spent so much of our time. She wasn't a regular churchgoer, but would come to events like VBS or some of the outings the church put together. We clicked almost instantly after meeting. Cynthia was everything I thought a young woman should be: intelligent, elegant, and confident. She carried herself with a kind of poise that made you want to sit up straighter just standing near her. Even my mom noticed it, jokingly calling her "Lady Di," comparing her to Princess Diana.

She had this vast vocabulary, which felt so impressive, and a way of carrying herself that was so refined. I looked at her and thought, *This is the kind of woman I want to be.* She had a big family like I did, but hers seemed healthier, more functional. Even when Cynthia moved on—first to UCLA and later to the Glendale area—we stayed in touch. The truth is, during those formative childhood years, I was looking for models. Children are natural mimics, absorbing behaviors, attitudes, and emotional cues from those around them. For those who grow up in unstable environments, the need to find a model becomes even more urgent. Psychologists call it *observational learning*. In stable homes, kids naturally model after their parents. But in chaotic or unpredictable environments, they'll look outward—toward teachers, older friends, or even fictional characters—to find templates for how to exist in the world.

For me, it meant forming friendships across different backgrounds, finding pieces of who I wanted to be in a patchwork of people. Some were kind and steady, showing me what warmth and encouragement looked like. Others had a toughness that, in a place like South Gate, seemed like the only way to get by. My upbringing taught me how to connect with all kinds of people—rich or poor, outgoing or reserved, Christian or secular. Growing up in a big family and spending so much time with cross-cultural friends teaches you to navigate different personalities. That skill can become a superpower in adulthood—walking into a room and feeling comfortable engaging with anyone there, regardless of status or demeanor.

One of the models I clung to early on was Wonder Woman, who was the epitome of everything I admired and longed for. Sure, I liked Hasselhoff on *Knight Rider* or Laura Ingalls—but *Wonder Woman* had it all. Beauty, confidence, strength. She always saved the day, and to a young girl who felt powerless much of the time, that was incredibly inspiring.

As for my real-life heroes, I didn't have to look further than the pulpit on Sunday morning, where Pastor Paul Bradshaw delivered his sermons, prayed for the sick, and prophesied over us. He truly displayed the heart of the Father. For all of my upbringing in California, we attended Lyn-Gate Neighborhood Church, which Pastor Paul and his wife Kathy, had recently joined after our former pastor stepped down. The church is still standing and holding regular services, sitting on the border of Lynwood and South Gate, in the heart of the inner city. It has since expanded to more cities in California as well as Mexico and other nations. The mission statement: We are a Christ-centered Acts 1:8 family of churches carrying on Christ's mission through church planting, Spanish ministry, Immigration Services, Urban Ministry, and Missions. Pastor Paul is still there at the helm, hair now grey with time, preaching week-in and week-out, approaching half a century of faithfully serving. My sister Rachel still attends and is active in the church. When I go back to California, I try to visit, even if it's only every couple of years. That church, with Pastor Paul at the helm, left an incredible mark on me.

Even as a child, I could see that Pastor Paul was a good and just man. He was a tall man of Irish descent with light brown hair and an air of quiet strength about him. He was not afraid to speak his mind, but he always did so with kindness and wisdom. He was a fatherly figure in many ways, and shepherded our family with care. It was evident that he poured his life into his calling. He wasn't just a figurehead at church; he was in the mix of our family's life. From officiating our weddings to showing up at the drop of a hat during tragedy, he embodied the full meaning of the word *pastor*. Knowing that most families in the area had limited means, he never asked for anything in return—literally. Whether it was weddings, funerals, or counseling, they always served selflessly without asking for a dime. The miracles of God were always evident in Pastor Paul's life, and there was always plenty of fruit to show.

On one occasion, when I was around eight, we attended VBS at the church. Justin and I were playing when he started chasing me, and I darted across the street—knowing I had been told *not* to cross the street under any circumstances. Just as I reached the other side, a car pulled up and a man got out, clearly intending to grab me. Pastor Paul, who had seen it all happen, was already on his way over. The moment the man saw him coming, the fear of God must've hit—he jumped back in his car and sped off. That was the kind of neighborhood we grew up in, and that moment became one of many where I recognized the divine hand of God protecting me, and Pastor Paul's critical role in our family life.

It's almost as though his impact on me is being felt just as much now as it was then. There are situations I find myself in where a decision needs to be made, and I reflect on something he would have said or done. The truth is, advice or input that's full of hot air doesn't last and dies in the ear of the listener. However, the word of God shared well acts like a perennial flower, growing up fresh year after year in perpetuity. I'm blessed to see the long-term fruit of what Pastor Paul and Kathy sowed.

The church community as a whole offered glimpses of stability in a world that often felt chaotic. We occasionally went to the beach as a congregation with baptisms and food. Our family also went to Christian camps—places like Canyon Meadows and Rolling J Ranch through Lyn-Gate Church. It broke up the routine and gave us a taste of community in a fresh way. I looked forward to these camping trips.

But even during those moments of joy, there was an undercurrent of confusion and disconnection that I couldn't quite shake as a kid. I somehow could *not* picture myself as an adult. My mind was fragmented and disconnected from any bigger picture or grandiose dream.

Fragmentation and disconnection became a childhood theme. My mother sent me to Arkansas during the summer when I was a child. I'm not sure how many times I visited, because I had completely blocked out the entire memory—except for one lone fragment: sitting in the back of a convertible car, eating ice cream. There was one summer trip in particular that always felt... off. I was around five years old, visiting my grandfather. The memory is cloudy, but there was a distinct heaviness—a sense that something had happened that didn't make sense. For years, I pushed it away, unable to understand why that visit left my spirit shattered in pieces.

What I didn't know then—and would only learn decades later—is that when a child experiences trauma that overwhelms their capacity to process it, part of their emotional development can freeze in time. According to Christian psychologists like Dr. Henry Cloud and Dr. John Townsend, unprocessed pain often causes people to become stuck at the developmental age when the trauma occurred. I didn't just forget what happened—I lost pieces of myself in that season. My growth in certain areas stalled, even as I matured chronologically. I would catch brief flashes of memory here and there, but nothing I could make sense of.

Then, as an adult in my fifties, God began to reveal more—bits and pieces through visions—until I finally understood why I had fragmented so deeply before I ever left kindergarten. A part of the little girl inside me had become emotionally and spiritually locked in a cage, buried deep in my subconscious. She would not be let out until I was half a century old.

Growing up in rough soil teaches you a lot about survival. It also leaves you clinging to a deep longing for stability and truth. When words don't line up with actions, when security feels like an illusion, you start to develop something like a sixth sense. That detector was Holy Spirit-given in part, but it was also forged through necessity.

As a child, the chaos I lived in pushed me to escape in the only way I knew how—daydreaming. I created a world in my head where things made sense, where families were loving, stable, and safe. My daydreams became a way to reclaim a sense of power, identity, and safety. Counseling later taught me the term *maladaptive daydreaming*, a survival mechanism where you create a better world in your mind to cope with the painful reality. In my fantasies, I had a voice. I was strong, seen, and heard—everything I was *not* in my own home.

One of the memories that still sits heavy in my heart came during third grade. I didn't have a decent pair of shoes for P.E., which took up about an hour of our school day. The only ones I had were old, tattered, and downright embarrassing. I flat-out refused to wear these beat-up hand-me-downs. The only alternative was a snug pair of flip-flops that I wore for months, simply because they were all I had.

One day during class, Mrs. Alexander pulled me aside and told me I'd need to start wearing tennis shoes if I wanted to keep participating in P.E. I went home filled with shame and hesitantly told my mom. Her response was short and final: She was unable to buy new shoes for me. *That was that.*

I didn't ask again—I already knew not to.

It broke something inside me. That event spun a web of thoughts: *How could I be worth so little that no one would buy me a pair of shoes?* That's when the daydreaming took over. I'd sit on the sidelines during P.E. and drift off into a world where I had everything—stylish Jordache jeans, beautiful shoes, and the kind of confidence that came from being seen and cared for. For an eight-year-old girl who felt invisible and powerless, it was more than fantasy—it was survival. My sister Rachel and I often didn't have what we needed, but we had each other. That bond of surviving together runs deep. Even now, we send each other clothes all the time—a reminder that we see each other, and that we've come a long way.

The term *dysregulated* perfectly captures how I felt emotionally as a child. Dysregulation showed up in my inability to manage my emotions or reactions. Looking back, I can see how this was the effect of my environment—very young parents, abandonment, and a lack of communication along the way. I simply couldn't process or release emotions in any healthy manner. If I lost in a neighborhood game, I'd take it so personally that I'd storm off and cry alone. The rejection would fall heavily upon me, and it was no longer about the game, but about the traces of abandonment in my soul. I didn't have a safe adult to talk to or help me regulate my nervous system, so I was left to chart the course alone. And seven-year-olds simply don't have the tools to do that.

Many kids experience moments of trauma, but when you don't have someone to comfort and validate you during those moments, the seeds of pain take root and the effects multiply. By the time I was 10, I'd already accumulated so many triggers that I was constantly on edge. This would clinically be described as *hypervigilance*, which is a state of increased alertness and heightened awareness to potential threats. It's a state where you are constantly scanning your environment for dangers, even when no real threat exists. Why? Because when no one steps in to help you process the pain, your body assumes it's up to you to stay safe—at all times, in all places. Your nervous system never powers down. It learns to live in a constant state of alert, always bracing for the next blow. For me, it meant I couldn't relax, couldn't trust, couldn't just *be a kid*. My mind was always calculating: *Who's upset? What's about to go wrong?* What can I do to avoid being the problem? Hypervigilance wasn't just a reaction—it became my way of being in the world. I suppressed much of my hypervigilance when I could, though, which is why my dysregulation didn't fully show up until my teenage years.

The benefit of hindsight is being able to see the patterns, the roots, the reasons. But as a child, my reality was that I had big emotions with nowhere to safely place them. My roots were searching, my petals stretching toward something brighter, something more stable, something true.

The cracks in your life's foundation might have limited you in some ways, but they forced you to dig deep in others. A street flower doesn't have acres of nutrient-rich soil to spread its roots. It doesn't have the luxury to sprawl far and wide. To bloom, it has to dig deep. It has to reach far below the surface, breaking through barriers that most never encounter. Its environment is harsh, the odds stacked against it, but the need to grow is greater than the obstacles.

CHAPTER TWO
Becoming Invisible

"I took you from the sheepfold, from following the sheep..."
(2 Samuel 7:8 NKJV)

"What's going on at home?"

Mrs. Alexander's voice was kind, but her question felt like a bucket of ice water on my head. I froze, my third-grade brain struggling to piece together an answer. She had pulled me aside after noticing I hadn't been turning in my homework, among other things, like constantly checking out and daydreaming. I was too young to articulate the chaos swirling in my life, but old enough to feel the weight of her question.

What *was* going on at home? I didn't have the words to explain, and even if I did, I wasn't sure I'd want to.

All I could think about in that instant was the shame. It wasn't just about the missing homework—it was a deeper realization that no one at home seemed to notice or care. Panicked, I blurted out the first thing that came to mind.

"There was a shooting in my neighborhood."

It wasn't a lie—just a convenient distraction. There *had* been a shooting up the street. A man had aimed at his girlfriend, and the story had spread through our small neighborhood like wildfire. I was exposed to stories of violence from a young age. I remember a house fire that killed a man down the street; the smell of smoke lingered in the air for days. But gruesome stories like that had nothing to do with my missing homework. I had simply learned—even by that age—that people tended to back off when confronted with something dramatic.

Mrs. Alexander looked startled, her kind eyes widening. She hesitated, then nodded and let the subject drop. I could feel the tight knot in my chest loosen. No parent-teacher conference. No awkward questions. Crisis averted—for now.

That moment exposed something about my life: Things were messy, and I instinctively tried to hide the mess. My ability to deflect started young, and I honed that skill for far too long. I had a growing sense of invisibility throughout my childhood years. Maybe I felt invisible because I didn't feel seen, or maybe I felt invisible because I was hiding—or both.

As for my mother, she was very young and lacked security herself, and as a result, she wasn't able to gift us kids with any. Reality felt fluid. What was true one day might change the next, depending on moods and whims. In hindsight, my mom was very wounded, and it was a miracle that she survived the harsh realities of her own upbringing.

Where my father's leaving destabilized me, the household culture that followed *demoralized* me. That is, until Greg came into the picture. He was the man who showed up when we needed him to. I first met Greg Kittleson when I was seven or eight. At the time, I didn't know he'd become a pillar in my life. He and my mom saw each other for a little over a year and when I was ten, they married. She was pregnant with my younger brother Philip at the time.

Greg was different: calm, steady, and deeply kind. He didn't speak in grandiose declarations or make promises he couldn't keep. He just showed up—and he stayed. He grew up on a farm in North Dakota, where life was simple but hard. He was no stranger to grit. As a young man, he decided to leave the plains behind and hitchhike to California, chasing opportunity and a fresh start. He'd tell stories about sitting on the side of the road, broke and hungry, and finding a $20 bill in the dirt after praying for provision. As a kid, I appreciated it when adults had the fruit to back up what they said, and Greg had it.

Once he arrived in California, Greg found work through a distant relative—Mike Pickett, my Aunt Nadine's husband. Mike owned a successful construction company and promised Greg a job if he made the trip. And so Greg left everything behind—including two children from a previous relationship in North Dakota—and started over.

It was through Nadine and Mike that Greg ended up at Lyn-Gate Neighborhood Church—which is where he strengthened his faith in God, and it's also where he met my mom—and us kids. At first, I didn't know what to make of Greg. None of us did. My brother Justin and I would whisper about him, trying to figure out his intentions. After all, we'd seen men come and go in our mom's life, each one leaving more damage than the last. Why should Greg be any different?

But Greg didn't try to force his way in. He just stayed consistent. He took us to Disneyland, organized camping trips, took us fishing, and made sure we had the kind of childhood adventures we didn't know we were missing. He wasn't much of a beach guy—but he loved being outdoors. As a family, we created more memories at campgrounds than on shorelines. Being a hunter and an NRA member, he opened us up to a new world of thought and perspective. Slowly but surely, his authenticity and kindness chipped away at our walls.

He worked as a brick mason, and I vividly remember him leaving the house at 5 a.m. every day, heading to job sites in a blue collar. He'd come home exhausted—without complaint. At the time, I didn't appreciate the weight of what that meant. But as I got older and entered the working world myself, I came to understand the magnitude of his sacrifice.

He didn't just teach us through his actions, though. Greg was a man of principles, and he had a saying for everything. His favorite? "If you're going to do something, do it right the first time." Greg believed in excellence—not for the sake of perfection, but because integrity demanded it. If something was worth doing, it was worth doing well.

Greg's marriage to my mom wasn't easy. She had been through a lot of pain, which left her guarded and fearful, and Greg's loving, adventurous nature often clashed with her self-protective walls. He never lashed out or raised his voice; he simply removed himself from the situation when discussions became too heated. Through it all, Greg stayed. And because of that, my siblings and I honor him even now. He didn't just marry my mom—he chose us. And while I carry a quiet sadness for his children in North Dakota, I'm beyond grateful for the man he was to us. He showed us what it meant to work hard, to love without conditions, and to live with integrity. At least in part, I owe much of my critical thinking to his influence. I recall as a kid asking, "Are we Democrat or Republican?"

My mom's response was: "I think we're Democrats."

Greg, on the other hand, would say, "Well, let's think about it..." He'd use real-life examples—like explaining the hypocrisy of people who criticize hunting game for meat while going through a McDonald's drive-thru to buy a hamburger. He'd break it all down in a way that made sense, and it stirred my critical thinking skills. He had a reputation for giving long lectures, which we'd roll our eyes at as kids. In hindsight, we see the value. While my relationship with my mom was complicated, there was one constant among my siblings: everyone had a ton of respect for Greg. He earned it.

Greg and my mom were creative and resourceful people. With a big blended family to support and one income, they had to be. If they couldn't buy it, they would build it. My mom used to sew clothes for us because thread is cheaper than new pants, which I thought was pretty special as a kid. Looking back, I know it *was* special. She'd buy patterns and fabric, and we'd get to choose the material, so it felt personal and unique. But in seventh grade, a classmate asked me—very pointedly and not kindly—where I got my outfit. Her tone made it clear that she was not curious or complimentary—but mocking. I connected the dots and realized that sewing our clothes was less about creativity and more about necessity. Then came a wave of shame and embarrassment, and a new thought: *Oh my gosh, we must be poor.*

I began noticing our neighbors who seemed better off, though I didn't fully understand why. There was a boy next door who was an only child, and his family always seemed to have more. They had a nice car and fewer restrictions. In contrast, we had an old van to accommodate all the kids. Greg earned a steady income—but with so many mouths to feed, each dollar gets accounted for pretty quickly. Before Greg, in particular, our meals were basic, and the menu didn't have much variety. No one ever taught our mom to cook; she had to figure it out on her own. Therefore, we had six or seven meals on repeat—mac and cheese, hamburgers, spaghetti, and meatloaf were staples. She did the best she could with a limited budget and no internet to turn to for inspiration.

Things changed a little when Greg entered the picture and introduced more variety into our meals. I still remember the first time he made clam chowder for us—it was from scratch, not a can, and it blew my mind. It was this "mystery food" we'd never had before, and I was in awe watching him whip it up. Sometimes, he'd bring back venison from a hunting trip, cook it with garlic, and make incredible meals. I appreciated that so much as a kid because it was such a departure from the usual options we had. We can joke about it today, as our mom has become creative and resourceful in the kitchen and enjoys cooking a variety of meals for the family.

Funny enough, the first crime I ever committed, breaking and entering, was food-related. I was 12 and my brother Justin was 13. By then, he had been running with a rough crowd who were older and wilder. They made trouble look fun, and Justin was all about it. One day, he convinced me to ditch school with him. He was a leader by nature, and I looked up to him. He had this magnetic pull, this way of making you want to follow him, even when you knew it wasn't the best idea.

We wandered the neighborhood for a while before Justin stopped in front of a modest stucco house, the kind you'd find on any street in Southgate. "Let's go inside," he said, grinning as if he were about to show me a magic trick.

"Inside? Why?" I asked, a little nervous.

"Come on," he said. "It'll be fun."

Before I knew it, we were climbing through a window he'd jimmied open. Inside, the house was quiet, the kind of stillness that makes you hold your breath. You'd think that Justin would have proceeded to search for jewelry or cash. Nope. I followed his steps to the kitchen, where he opened the fridge like he owned the place and pulled out a few items.

"What are you doing?" I whispered, glancing nervously toward the door.

"Making a sandwich," he said casually, as if breaking into someone's home to raid their fridge was the most normal thing in the world.

For Justin, this wasn't about taking anything valuable; it was about the thrill. It was about saying, *I can*. But the thrill didn't last long. Somehow, either that night or the next day, the police found us. Maybe it was a paper we left behind—an old test or worksheet from school with one of our names scrawled on it. Maybe it was something Justin said to someone who couldn't keep a secret. Either way, the homeowners reported the break-in, and we got caught.

The police didn't arrest me, but they took me to the station to scare me—and they accomplished that goal. Justin, on the other hand, had a record. I didn't know the full extent of it at the time—he was good at keeping me in the dark—but I knew enough to understand that this time, he wasn't going to come home with us. It would be his first stint in juvenile detention.

When my mom picked me up, her anger wasn't directed at Justin. It was taken out on me. She blamed me for the break-in, as if I'd dragged him into it instead of the other way around. Sadly, this shift in blame wasn't an isolated incident, but a trend. The household dynamic between each sibling was drastically different. Some siblings were treated with consistent kindness, favor, and generosity—gifts, praise, a sense of belonging. For others, it was anything but that. It wasn't just a matter of occasional neglect—but a clear divide. It was reminiscent of something straight out of *Cinderella*. As adults looking back at childhood, each of us kids had a very different experience growing up—as if we were born into different households. We had a shared roof but not a shared experience. One sibling might rave about her childhood while the other can demonstrate a string of bruises. Rachel and I bonded often because we were both treated in a similar manner.

Justin, the oldest boy, was incapable of wrongdoing. His need to belong led him into trouble. He was smart—so smart that he got bored easily, which often led to bad decisions. He wanted to belong, to feel important, and, without a strong father figure early in life to guide him, he sought that belonging in all the wrong places. At the same time, Justin was my protector, but he was also a boy who needed protecting. For a long time, I didn't know how to reconcile those two realities.

Even though he was just 11 months older than me, and growing up, people often thought we were twins, I gravitated to Justin as a father figure. He had a voice when I didn't, and I craved the sense of belonging I thought he had. He was protective and strong—those traits bloomed early. One day, when we were about eight years old, we were playing a game with some neighborhood kids, including a boy named Louis and a girl named Alicia. It was an innocent, sunny afternoon. At some point, Louis leaned in and kissed me—just a harmless, childish peck, but before I could even react, Justin was on him.

"That's my sister!" he shouted, punching Louis square in the face.

The rest of us froze. Louis stood there holding his face, looking more stunned than hurt. And me? I felt this strange mix of embarrassment and pride. My brother had defended me, and for weeks, it became the neighborhood story: "Did you hear what Justin did? He punched Louis for kissing Sandi!"

He offered a safety that I didn't find just anywhere. It's one of the reasons I've always been drawn to powerful figures—people who seem to command their lives with strength and purpose. Winston Churchill, for example, has always fascinated me. Here was a man who didn't care what anyone thought. He smoked cigars, drank port for dinner, and snapped back at Lady Astor with clever retorts that would make anyone blush. But beyond his sharp tongue and larger-than-life personality, Churchill was steadfast in his mission. He carried the weight of saving a nation—and in many ways, the world—with a sense of duty that I deeply admire.

Part of my admiration for people in that mold comes from the contrast to my own life growing up. I didn't have a voice to influence and problem-solving abilities. I felt I *was* the problem. I was constantly trying to avoid trouble or keep the peace, all while internalizing a belief that my worth was tied to how well I could stay out of trouble and out of sight.

*　*　*

Here's the thing about being invisible: you're not just unseen by others, but you are invisible to yourself. I had no idea who I was or what I was capable of. Instead of striving for greatness, I focused my energy on making sure I didn't get in the way. In my mind, I wasn't the hero of the story. I was the quiet extra in the background, doing my best not to disrupt the scene.

What I did not know at the time was that God has a habit of using the hidden and the obscure. When we first meet Gideon in Judges 6, he's threshing wheat in a winepress—hiding from the Midianites. Why does that matter? Because threshing wheat typically involved separating the grain from the chaff by beating it and tossing it into the air in an open area so the wind could blow the chaff away. This was usually done on a massive threshing floor for collection—in an open, elevated space exposed to the wind.

However, because of the enemy raids, Gideon couldn't afford to be seen out in the open. Instead, he did the job hidden, with a small winepress in a cave. He isn't standing tall, preparing to lead Israel into victory. He's crouching, trying to stay out of sight, invisible to the enemy and himself. So when the angel of the Lord appears and greets him with "The Lord is with you, mighty warrior," it feels like a mistake (see Judges 6:12).

Mighty warrior? Gideon didn't see himself that way. He protests immediately: "Pardon me, my lord, but how can I save Israel? My clan is the weakest in Manasseh, and I am the least in my family" (see Judges 6:15). He's not just invisible—he's convinced he's *insignificant*.

The fight for significance is universal in the human story. We all want it, and in God's economy, we all have it. But we are not all *affirmed* that we have it. I didn't have the tools to see my potential as a kid. Similar to Gideon, I believed a narrative about myself that I was the least of the least. And like him, I tried to stay small, hidden, and safe.

But what strikes me about Gideon's story is how God responds. He doesn't argue with Gideon or try to convince him that he's great. Instead, He says, "Go in the strength you have…Am I not sending you?" (Judges 6:14). God saw something in Gideon that Gideon couldn't see in himself, and He called it out. He didn't wait for Gideon to feel ready or strong or qualified. He simply asked Gideon to trust Him and take the first step. Gideon wasn't a warrior because he felt like one; he became a warrior because God called him one.

God was with me in my "winepress" moments, even when I felt small and invisible. He wasn't limited by my perception of myself. I may have been hidden to others and hidden to myself, but I was right in the center of God's eye. The question isn't whether we're capable—it's whether we're willing to trust the One who is.

Even as a child, I had a heart for God and valued compassion and kindness. I loved people deeply and built friendships easily. Community was important to me—I loved being part of something larger than myself. And yet, the first community we ever experience is the one we're born into: *family*. For better or worse, it's in that setting where we begin to learn how to see ourselves, how to navigate relationships, and how to understand our place in the world.

From abandonment to emotional guessing games, my first community gave me a template that colored the rest of my story. The lessons we internalize in our first community bleed into the way we see every other one. A child who grows up feeling loved and validated is more likely to approach friendships, workplaces, and church communities with confidence and a default sense of acceptance. But when your foundation is marked by instability or rejection, you carry those wounds with you. It shapes how you connect with others—or how you don't. For those with abandonment issues, you can find yourself either desperately clinging to relationships or cutting and running before you have a chance to be hurt again.

As I moved into adolescence and began forging my way into other communities—high school, new friend groups, work—those early impressions from my upbringing followed me. Not only that, but as a person comes of age, the innocent struggles such as shyness or hiding can manifest in ways that have much higher stakes and more severe consequences. I was hopeful that my teenage years would bring a sense of independence and happiness—but time would tell whether or not that hope was in vain.

CHAPTER THREE

Think Again

"Adolescence is a time in which you experience everything more intensely." —Edward Zwick

When your childhood is difficult, it can cause you to grow up quickly—not necessarily because you are some mature and responsible prodigy, but because you desperately need a change of scenery. As soon as I was able, I had my first job, my first car, and started handling my own purchases. Independence was a sort of cure for my childhood.

Even then, there were countless lessons to learn as I came of age. On one occasion, I had gone into an auto parts store to buy brake pads for my car, which was sitting in the drive. When the clerk gave me my change, I walked out of the store thinking I had just scored an unexpected payday. Instead of giving me back the correct amount, he handed me fifty dollars instead of thirty.

To a teenager, that extra twenty bucks hit like a jackpot. I didn't think twice about where it came from, what it meant for the cashier, or the fact that it wasn't mine. But when I got home and casually mentioned the mix-up, Greg gently but firmly explained that I needed to think again.

"Sandi, if you keep that money, the cashier's drawer will come up short and he'll have to cover that out of his own paycheck."

My unexpected blessing turned into a burden on my conscience. Greg didn't scold me. He simply said, "Let's go back and make it right."

Together we walked the few blocks back to the store, and I returned the money. My selfish excitement, which became guilt, had now become peace as I forked the money over to a grateful clerk. It was the school of integrity, and Greg was the headmaster.

When I picture that era in the early '80s, I imagine the stonewashed jeans replacing the bell-bottoms of the prior generation, with wild hair and neon everywhere. Mom loved The Beach Boys and Linda Ronstadt, so those records were always playing in the house. All the kids and teens knew each other, and our parents were all on a first-name basis.

By the time I became a teenager, South Gate's decline was in its final form, though. Where cops once stopped to check on us and offer some baseball cards, they were now following and frisking my older brother and looking for criminal activity—which they often found. The innocent kids became suspects, and I knew I wanted to get out of South Gate someday, but didn't know how or what it would look like.

On the home front, the family grew. By 1983, Greg and my mom welcomed our little brother Phillip into the mix. Then Priscilla was born in 1987 and Aaron in 1991—making us a family of nine, with seven kids born over a nearly 20-year span. The age gap was real, but I grew to love and cherish my new little siblings. Practically speaking, there is less attention to go around with so many kids in the house. By then, I had pretty well given up on being a stand-out in the home and started mingling with less-than-savory crowds.

By the time I was fifteen, I had been introduced to alcohol and it became a somewhat routine experience. It wasn't as though there was one pivotal moment where I made a conscious decision to party—I just sort of slipped into it. House parties were a regular thing, and I certainly partook. The idea of self-medicating came naturally. I would go to these weekend parties regularly, sometimes dragging Rachel along with me.

Justin, my older brother, had his own crowd—an even rougher one by then. His friends were into gang activity, and while I wasn't about that life, I was drawn to the social scene. I wanted connection, a sense of belonging. I sought emotional nourishment.

To put my emotional lack in perspective, I don't think I received a proper hug from my mother until I turned eighteen. Which, by then—with almost two decades of affectionless relationship between us—was super awkward. Greg would occasionally drop an "I love you," but my mom wasn't able at the time.

And yet, for some reason, I became warm and expressive in social settings. Maybe I craved it so badly that I became overly affectionate with friends to compensate.

For years, Justin had been a kind of buffer between us and our mom, but when he wasn't around, Rachel and I bore the brunt of her unpredictability. Yes, faith played a major role in our upbringing, but we often saw a version of faith that left us more confused than if we hadn't been exposed to faith to begin with.

For instance, when Rachel and I were early teenagers, our mom sat us down one day and told us something that shook us to our core. She said they had heard from God that both she and Greg were going to die in a car accident during an upcoming trip to Northern California for Thanksgiving.

The news left us breathless. More than just the fear of losing our parents, it was the burden placed on us next that overwhelmed us: "When we die, you girls will need to take care of your younger siblings."

We were terrified. That night, and many after, Rachel and I lay awake wondering what we would do. *Who would take us in? Who would help us raise the others?* We even talked about Pastor Paul, hoping maybe he would step in if the worst really happened. But mostly, we carried this quiet fear and a heavy sense of responsibility—children ourselves, trying to imagine how we'd survive alone.

And then...the trip came and went. Nothing happened. It was never open for discussion. And we didn't dare ask. There was a deep confusion and a kind of quiet shame we didn't have the tools to name.

Looking back, I can see how that moment marked the beginning of a quiet unraveling of trust. I started to notice that what people said did not always align with what actually happened. At the time, I couldn't articulate it—I just knew that the ground beneath me didn't always feel steady.

Years later, my mom made a passing comment about dying and me needing to take care of the younger kids. It instantly triggered fear and terror, and something in me snapped. Without thinking, I blurted out, "I'm not going to take care of them if something happens to you!"

She swiftly slapped me across the face. Hard.

The sound and the sting of it reinforced what I already knew—truth was dangerous. Speaking up came with consequences. I had spent so much of my childhood swallowing my feelings, accepting responsibility that wasn't mine, and believing things that did not make sense. Exploring boundaries as a teenager often triggered the same abrupt and harsh punishment.

In hindsight, this very instance birthed my love for justice and truth. It made me the genuine person I am today and shaped what I stand for. It created in me a love for the redemptive power of God to right the wrongs in the world, especially those who are broken and hurting.

I wasn't the only one trying to make sense of the tension in our home. There was a time when my sister Rachel bore the weight of being unfairly blamed for things beyond her control. I remember a season when our washing machine started tearing holes in our clothes—small rips that kept showing up, no matter what we did. Instead of recognizing the real issue, my mom, perhaps exhausted or overwhelmed, directed her frustration at Rachel. She insisted Rachel was somehow responsible.

It wasn't the first time she'd been singled out this way, and I imagine how confusing and painful that must have been for her.

It wasn't just that—my mom had been building up this narrative that Rachel was mentally unstable for months. The worst of this narrative culminated in an attempt to check Rachel into a facility called McClaren Hall in Los Angeles that housed children with severe mental health issues.

I'll never forget the day my dad, with visible reluctance, drove Rachel to an intake appointment. He sat with the intake worker, who quickly recognized that Rachel didn't belong there. She wasn't mentally ill—she was a deeply hurting teenager, carrying more than her share of trauma. My dad brought her back home, but the experience had already left its mark. In hindsight, I truly believe it was God's grace that protected her. Years later, McClaren Hall was shut down amid reports of abuse and neglect.

One morning after the fiasco, Rachel came to me and said, "I can't take this anymore. Let's run away."

I couldn't argue. So we packed our things—whatever we could fit in a laundry basket—and snuck out of the house through a side window. We didn't have anywhere to go, so we ended up at a friend's house just a couple of blocks away.

Other times, we stayed with a woman from our church named Lisa. She had such a motherly way about her, but she was also firm. I remember her making us lunch and sitting us down, saying she'd have to call our parents and let them know where we were.

Our grandmother, Mercedes, later told us that she had offered to take Rachel in when things were particularly bad, even preparing a room for her. My mom never followed through. When Rachel found out about this years later, it broke her heart. She had wanted so badly to go to a place where she felt loved and valued, and Grandma Mercy would have provided that.

Nevertheless, we grinded through our upbringing, running away when we could, returning when we must. We never stayed gone for more than a few days. Our parents would call Pastor Paul, and he would drive around the neighborhood looking for us. He knew what was happening at home, but there was only so much he could do. When he found us, he never lectured or shamed us. Instead, he was calm, understanding, and kind—offering encouragement and truth without judgment.

Since I couldn't turn to anyone at home, I found refuge in others. My Aunt Nadine, Aunt Allison, and later my Aunt Dawn became safe havens. Nadine was my dad's sister, Dawn was my mom's half-sister, and Allison had married into my mom's side of the family. She later divorced my uncle due to abuse, so she understood firsthand what it was like to live with instability.

These three women played a critical role in my life. They were the ones who spoke encouragement over me. They told me I was smart, that I could accomplish anything. They believed in God's word and reflected that in their conversations.

Allison, especially, was a source of comfort when I turned 18. At one point, home wasn't a safe place to live, so I stayed with her and my two cousins for a couple of months. She never pressured me or made me feel like a burden—she simply offered a safe place to land and a comforting, listening heart. She gave me exactly what a wounded teenager needed: unconditional love. I was drawn to her like a moth to a warm and steady flame.

Even writing about it now, I feel the weight of how those years impacted me. It wasn't just poor parenting—it was emotional abuse. And it wasn't just a single traumatic event—it was a pattern of instability, manipulation, and neglect. It left me confused, burdened, and desperate for healing.

When I needed affirmation, I was met with blame. Someone with narcissistic tendencies will undermine your experience, rather than *validate* your experience. Validation was a concept that was not understood nor made manifest anywhere near the walls of our home. I spent much of my childhood feeling like I was in the way of my mother—like an inconvenience she had to manage rather than a daughter she wanted to nurture.

I still grieve for that little girl who was forced to carry so much. If I were watching this happen to someone else, my heart would break for them. So why wouldn't I allow myself the same grace? Acknowledging your pain doesn't mean you're stuck in it. It means you're choosing to heal from it.

It's worth noting that when writing about pain from my upbringing, it's not from a place of bitterness or woundedness. I don't hold resentment toward my mother. I've walked through healing, through forgiveness, through years of allowing God to mend what was broken—which we will unpack in more detail in chapters to come. But this is my story. And telling my story means telling the truth—not to hurt or blame, but to state the fullness of my testimony with *honesty*.

For a long time, I felt like I had to protect others from my reality and that sharing my experiences would be dishonoring. But silence doesn't heal wounds in myself or others. In fact, secrets make you sick.

I've spent a lot of time trying to understand my mother's behavior. When she told us she would soon die, was it attention-seeking? Was she trying to elicit a response, to feel needed? The story I tell myself is, at some level, she wanted reassurance. Perhaps she wanted us to say, "No, Mom, don't worry. We'll take care of everything if you pass," or even stir up a fearful, "Please don't die; we need you!"

She definitely had a way of reinforcing a certain role for me—the caretaker. As long as I was cleaning, babysitting, and taking care of everyone else, I had value in her eyes. And as a child, when someone tells you your worth is tied to what you *do* instead of who you *are*, you are set up for a life of striving and performance-based love.

I understand now that my mom actually needed the help, and God provided grace to see me through.

I see my mom differently now. When I look at her, I don't see a strong adult who is an evil person. I see the little girl who was abandoned and deeply wounded. And when you have unhealed trauma like that, your brain doesn't process things the way it should. Every rejection, every moment of feeling unwanted—it sends you right back to that original wound. As a result, you take it out on those near you—even if those near you are your own children.

It wasn't intentional cruelty on her part, nor do I think she was out to get me or Rachel. It was simply brokenness doing what brokenness does.

We cannot give what we do not have, and generations of emotional bankruptcy were playing out in my family lines. I remember thinking, *I will never be that controlling. I will never be that fearful. I will never let my pain make my world so small.* It was a quiet vow I made, even as a child, and one I carried into adulthood.

What I did not grasp was that a quiet, frustrated vow could be a prophecy in the mouth of a child. If I had held on to that inner vow in my own strength, I would have ended up repeating the cycle of pain in my own life.

Whether the person who hurt you ever repents and gets healed—that does not determine whether or not you can find healing and freedom.

Today, I understand that Jesus died for my mother's struggles just as much as He died for mine. I'm deeply grateful that He didn't withhold His love—His sacrifice was for all of us, without condition. And He calls us to love in that same radical way.

Though the journey has been anything but easy, I can now say with a whole heart that I truly forgive my mother. Through much healing, I've learned to forgive freely, just as I have been forgiven. If I didn't, I'd risk becoming like the unforgiving servant Jesus spoke of in Matthew 18:21–35.

Does this passage on the unforgiving servant mean that we live without boundaries? Of course not—forgiveness doesn't mean forgetting or ignoring boundaries. It means choosing mercy over bitterness. And even with necessary distance, you can still extend love and kindness to those who once caused you pain.

* * *

A wreck. This is the only appropriate two-word response to the question, "What were you like as a teenager?"

Unsure of myself and blind to the future, I believed in God but had little trust in any sort of destiny. Life was not something you *lived* but something that just happened to you. I coped with parties and drinking—a social Novocaine for the soul. Resorting to being the class clown, I pushed boundaries and did anything for a laugh or appreciation. One particular forbidden party comes to mind.

My first job at 15 was at Pizza Hut and initially, I was a great employee: hardworking, reliable, and thrilled to earn my own cash. I kept that job for a couple of years, but at a certain point, my decision-making wasn't exactly stellar. One night, after a football game, I got the brilliant idea to take a couple of friends back to Pizza Hut. I had the keys, so we let ourselves in, made some pizzas, and drank a few beers.

At the time, it felt daring, fun, and innocent. The next week, when I got fired, it felt regrettable, stupid, and not worth it.

The manager, Jose, was a bit of a character himself. He wasn't exactly a rule-follower either and often bent the rules to suit himself. In fact, he admitted during our conversation that if it were up to him alone, he would've let it slide. But because someone else in management found out, he had no choice but to fire me.

"Look, Sandi, I know it was you. The trash you guys left behind kind of gave it away," he said.

I quickly got another job at a pizza parlor down the street, and when my parents asked what happened to the Pizza Hut job, I told them I needed a gig "closer to home."

They rarely asked questions.

I wound up getting my sister Rachel a job there as well. One night, we stopped by the store in the middle of a double date. It was late, and while parked, someone approached us all with a gun. They demanded the keys, and we handed them over without question. We were being carjacked.

In those days, people would approach you as you were getting into your car, use a weapon to intimidate you, and take your vehicle for a joyride or party. They'd usually ditch the car within a couple of days.

That was exactly what happened. We were shaken but unharmed. After calling the police, we had to call our parents to explain. Instead of concern or relief, my mom proceeded to scold us for being late.

The gun in our face? Nothing worth mentioning. Broken curfew? That's the real issue at hand.

Rachel and I laugh about it now.

The car was found abandoned a few days later.

Not all trauma is created equal. Some can be laughed at in time, like a curfew-breaking carjack. Some trauma is a slow drip of cruel patterns that builds walls inside of you. Other trauma is sudden, severe, and divides your life into a "before" and "after" the incident.

At sixteen, one such traumatic event occurred. Per usual, I had gone to a party and drank too much. Vulnerable and helpless by that point, two guys took me to a home and took advantage of me.

For years, I carried the weight of that night in silence. It wasn't until much later, through inner healing sessions, that I began to process it. The trauma had left parts of me—my mind, my body, my spirit—disconnected. I couldn't even look at myself in the mirror without clothes on because I felt so detached from my own body. I didn't want anything to do with myself.

Imagine someone cuts their finger preparing a dish, and with blood pouring everywhere, they ask, "Is it bad?"

A standard response is, "Just don't look at it."

Why? Because we want to shield the victim from further trauma. We do this internally with our own selves also. That kind of dissociation from trauma, I've learned, is simply how we attempt to survive.

But surviving isn't the same as living. I had to go back and integrate that sixteen-year-old girl into the woman I am today. I had to reclaim my body, my spirit, my sense of self, and my voice.

More on that later.

Trauma in the home and outside the home began to birth a deep-seated anger within me. Outside of my home, it would boil and spill over in unpredictable ways. I recall when Priscilla was being bullied by a neighborhood girl, and I took it upon myself to step in—making a few threats and pushing the girl.

I remember punching a girl who tried to bully me in school. She fought back, and it turned into a full-on scuffle. Later into my teen years, I mellowed out a little, but was still mouthy. I had a sharp tongue, and I wasn't afraid to use it.

As my teen years were coming to a close, I had to formulate a plan for the years to come. The problem was, I didn't have much vision for my future.

Academics were not exactly a priority, given the context I was living in. My GPA sat somewhere between a B and a C—neither parent hovering over us about homework. Greg focused on instilling values rather than micromanaging report cards.

I had an inkling that life would somehow work itself out, but my home environment wasn't exactly an incubator for inspiration.

It's true that vision often comes from outside of ourselves, and obtaining that vision often means changing environments. I planned to do just that.

As high school came to a close, I enrolled at Cerritos College in Norwalk, making the choice to study business. It was something I had a natural interest in, and I appreciated the idea of creating something, building an organization, or turning a profit.

New studies, new jobs, new settings—all meant new possibilities, but also new challenges. Changing environments can expose you to new vision, but it doesn't necessarily erase the patterns you've carried with you.

I was stepping into adulthood with more freedom than ever before—but freedom without direction can feel just as brutal as captivity.

CHAPTER FOUR
Toxic Ownership

"The Lord directs our steps, so why try to understand everything along the way?" (Proverbs 20:24 NLT)

Growth is not linear. We would like to think that our spiritual, mental, and emotional growth follow a perfect path, angling up steadily until we eventually depart this life. The truth is, growth and healing can have peaks and valleys, spurts and interruptions, promotions and delays. As I left home and moved to a small apartment in Norwalk to attend school, it's not as though my life did a complete 180 with a glorious upward trend to the image of Christ. Sure, my environment changed, but reinventing my interior environment would take time.

There exists a myth of instant adulthood in society. It's as though turning 18, moving out, or paying your own light bill automatically makes you an adult. The truth is, maturity isn't about a number or chronological milestone—it's about wisdom, accountability, and responsibility. We all could point to 60-year-old individuals who still have the emotional makeup of a child.

Whether we are curing a broken upbringing or continuing a legacy of wholeness, our job is to partner with Jesus who is the architect of our souls. He is the foreman who provides the plans, and we are the co-laborers yielding to His construction in and around us. Maturity doesn't happen because we keep on breathing, it happens because we keep on building.

But what happens when you've been building from blueprints of pain? What happens when the foundation of your life has been shaped by expectations that were never yours to carry?

Even though I was legally an adult, making it on my own, I had plenty of inner formation that still needed to take place. Freedom without discipline can be destructive, and while I knew I wouldn't step off the deep end, I also wasn't fully free. Because deep down, I was still trying to fill a role that was never mine to play.

Being blamed for Justin's break-in or slapped for not wanting to raise my siblings in the event of my parents' deaths all caused something in me called a *parental inversion*. This is when a child takes on duties that usually belong to the parent. Beyond your basic anxiety and depression, this sort of inversion can cause a slew of other issues. One, it robs you of your childhood. When a little girl should be playing with Barbies and dreaming of the future, she is wrapped up in laundry, dishes, and constantly trying to avoid a mistake that might upset the fragile balance in the home.

Long-term, it instilled in me a belief that it was my job to fix everyone and everything. Delegating responsibility grated against everything in me. For example, things like asking for help to move were as painful as pulling teeth.

I became the "hero" in relationships, always stepping in to save others, whether they needed it or not. It was exhausting, but I didn't know any other way to be. As I navigated my early adulthood, I found myself walking on phantom eggshells. In dating, I saw potential partners as projects to fix not people to know. At work, I learned to do everything myself, because deep down, I felt that handing over a task was a liability, and no one would do the job as well as I would.

Jocko Willink's book *Extreme Ownership* has become a popular concept, encouraging people to take responsibility for their lives and their teams. The heart of the message is sound and much-needed in our culture today. As I was entering adulthood, however, I had passed beyond *extreme* ownership and stepped into what I would call *toxic* ownership. I wasn't just responsible—I was responsible for people and things that God never meant for me to carry. I trained myself to be *needless* and *wantless*—which is a coping mechanism known in the therapeutic world. Culture often celebrates us for being independent, needing no one. Our modern-day heroes and icons are often seen alone and pride themselves on having dependence on themselves and their own work ethic only.

As with just about any psychological glitch that needs healing, there can be a silver lining. In my case, I did not lack work ethic and have never been shy about putting in the hours. Greg's example growing up certainly helped too. As soon as I got to Cerritos College, I pulled out the paper, checked the classifieds, and started landing side jobs to support myself while getting an associate's degree.

I made some new friends, bounced around the area, and found time to party and drink while studying. Sadly, the self-medication I discovered in high school continued through the next few years. When I could swing it, I would take ski trips to Northern California, hitting the slopes in Tahoe or Mammoth with my cousins and Aunt Allison. It took me longer than two years to finish my associate's degree, as I was juggling odd jobs, trying to stay afloat. Some kids have a path that's pushed on them—doctor, lawyer, consultant. I had none of that, which wasn't a bad thing. Greg was supportive, and as the kids got older, I could see his sense of pride in us grew. Because of my strained relationship with my mother, she wasn't someone I confided in for career advice. Even as time went on and my faith deepened, I recall mentioning to her that I was in the middle of reading *Ever Increasing Faith*, from the great British evangelist Smith Wigglesworth. Her reaction was immediately dismissive: "You don't have his anointing."

So naturally, I learned to not fall at her feet to beg for support. Where vision and encouragement were lacking back home, I started to sense it while living on my own. I finally got out and started spending time with people who had vision and purpose for their lives. Being in healthy environments allowed me to dream again.

While I would go back and attend Lyn-Gate Church here and there, I wasn't exactly on fire for Jesus in my early twenties. By the time I hit age 25, I realized I needed to do a little more growing up. I wanted stability, to find a place without roommates, and to take new steps in independence. I got my heart right with God as best I could and prayed for a stable, long-term, full-time job.

I submitted my resume to a commercial refrigeration firm located just south of downtown Los Angeles, which at the time was not a good area. On the day of the interview, there were two candidates—myself and another lady. When the other lady arrived and saw a homeless man sleeping at the front door of the office, she felt the location was not for her and took off, which meant I had my first professional job outside of college. The person who interviewed me stated that she had never seen a homeless person near the building—that was a very rare experience. I knew that a Divine hand was once again upon my life.

It turned out to be one of the most stabilizing jobs I ever had. I worked in the accounting department, taking care of payroll, handling receiving, and generating proposals for the sales team. I had found a small studio apartment nearby and had a fresh motivation in my soul. It was the first time I felt a true sense of community outside of my siblings. The women in that office, especially one older lady named Jean, took me under their wing.

Being in a safe place had an adverse effect on me at times. I would occasionally call in sick, feeling undone at the safety of this small department. I could be myself, and nobody in the office brought any assumptions to the table about me. I wrestled with the vulnerability that came with that. I was uncovering what's called a *disorganized attachment*, which is the push-pull of fear and longing. For a child, they might seek comfort from a caregiver but then immediately pull away for fear of abandonment. As an adult, because I feared abandonment, I feared intimacy. I was accustomed to not knowing where I stood—sometimes I was accepted, sometimes I wasn't. Relationships felt unpredictable, which means they felt threatening. So as an adult, I built walls, struggling to open up, and keeping new people at arm's length.

People who meet me today might be surprised to learn that for most of my life, I rarely showed outward emotions. My subconscious had been trained to believe that emotions made you vulnerable, and vulnerability led to pain. It wasn't until my forties, after years of intentional healing, that I was finally able to break free from that. Nevertheless, in that precious office environment, God set me up with a sanctuary where healing could start to happen. My walls were being chipped away, and the Lord was setting me up to become who I had always been. I sought anchors like this because adulthood was proving just as challenging as childhood.

By then, my siblings were all going in different directions with their lives. Most were good, some bad. My older brother Justin was raised without much discipline and lived his life that way, even into adulthood. It was the early 2000s, and it was clear his life was going in a direction that I could not support him in. At the same time, I felt responsible for him and his mistakes. On one occasion, he called for help—not because he earnestly needed a hand, but because he had committed a serious crime and was looking for an escape hatch.

I had to put my foot down. "I'm sorry, I cannot help you, Justin."

Eventually, he quit calling. Less than a year later, I was driving home from work and passed a Mexican restaurant we used to go to as kids. It prompted me to call my mom. The voice I heard on the other end was broken and panicked—she informed me that she just got news that Justin had died. He was committing a crime in Arizona, and when a state trooper showed up, Justin had fired on the cop. The return fire ended Justin's life.

The shock and anguish of the situation was immediate. I felt an intense pain, but also a *shame* that was just as penetrating.

Through the funeral and arrangements, I kept myself emotionally distant from the reality of what happened. I grieved the best I knew how, which was not all that well because shame kept the event in a sealed box somewhere deep in my soul. He was such a smart young man with endless potential, yet here he was, squandering it. Our adventures as children, hand in hand, were a distant memory and replaced by this final scene in his life that I simply wanted to forget. Could I have done something more? Would anything have worked? I ran from the questions and kept my mind on other things—hoping the grief would not resurface with interest later.

* * *

As my twenties came and went, I ramped up my involvement in church. Being further from Lyn-Gate, I got involved in a church closer to home and work in Los Angeles. It was a bit of a rough church, to say the least. Congregants were not showing up in Range Rovers nor tithing on their trust funds each week. The pastor had been in and out of prisons and in a gang before coming to Jesus.

After getting saved, he wanted to do something for the Los Angeles area and hit the streets, preaching to the lost and broken gang members of Hollywood. Eventually, this led to the formation of a small church, Hope Harvest, and, in due course, I found out about it and showed up one Sunday.

The church was intense. From a doctrinal standpoint, they believed much the same as the church I grew up in: Jesus is Lord, and He is still actively speaking and doing miracles. The difference between Lyn-Gate and this new church was in attitude and tone. While it might not have been spoken out loud, it felt like if you left their church, you were essentially outside of God's favor. There was a tribalistic edge that came through in the culture of the church.

After everything I had been through, I was desperate for stability, desperate to do the right thing, and to be in the right place. And when someone in authority indicates that you are on some of the only *safe* spiritual ground, you plant yourself in that ground—which I did.

Still quite broken, I plugged into the church, joined the drama team, and forged friendships. I overlooked some of the dogma because, frankly, I felt as if I belonged. By then, I felt I had achieved some sense of stability—I wasn't partying or drinking and I had a vision for the future, but in reality, I wasn't whole. Shortly, I met a man named Eric who had been attending the church. He had a past of his own, and, similar to me, was looking for a community.

When Eric and I started dating, we realized that the church had a very dogmatic approach to courtship. Archaic ideas about dating with a chaperone present were prescribed, and, to two independent adults, it felt insane. As a result, we fell out of the graces of the church.

I spent the next several months getting to know Eric. He had a kind heart, which I noticed first, and reminded me a bit of Greg—steady, hardworking, and responsible. What really drew me in, though, was his closeness to his family. He came from a tight-knit home and his parents were still together, something I wasn't used to seeing.

We didn't date long—only about eight months before we got married.

When recalling a season of life such as this, I want to be delicate with the details. Disclosure is sometimes viewed as *dishonor*, and I want to carefully recall this season in an honorable way. We were young, definitely didn't ask the right questions, and were ultimately in over our heads. Looking back, I think I mistook his family's stability for his own. He had struggled with addiction before we met, but by the time I knew him, he had cleaned up his life, gone through a men's home, and was studying the Bible consistently. He had even preached a few times at church, and in my mind, I thought, *Here's a godly man, a family man, someone who has overcome his past and is moving forward.*

At the time, it all felt right on track, especially in a church like Hope Harvest, where they emphasized quick courtships and getting married young. Of course, in hindsight, I realize how little I actually knew about him before making the leap into matrimony. I certainly was in no place to enter into a relationship during that time on my journey either.

After getting married, we moved to Lynwood and did what couples do—we built a life together, went to church, spent time with his family, and adjusted to the new rhythm. But over time, I started to notice cracks in the foundation. Eric had a hard time opening up emotionally.

Coming home from work, I would hope for some kind of meaningful interaction, but usually found him playing video games or watching wrestling with his friends. If his family planned a trip, we went. If they had a gathering, we were there. But there was no real "us."

Things reached a point where I felt lonelier in marriage than I ever had when I was single. Of course, I had no grid for diagnosing issues, and I couldn't forge a path of communication between us on my own. At one point, I took a job in Orange County, working for a welfare-to-work program. There, I was surrounded by people who were learning and growing, people who were rebuilding their lives. As part of my training, I had to go through the same personal development courses that we would be teaching to clients.

One day, I sat in a session about growth and expansion. The speaker explained how when a person grows and their heart and mind expand, it makes it impossible to go back to where they were before. The idea struck me. I had been growing, I had been expanding, but if I was being honest, my husband wasn't. A new thought occurred to me at that moment: *We're never going to make it.*

That night, I went home and tried to talk to him about it. I told him that I wanted more—not more money, not more security, but more "us." I wanted real closeness and growth *together*. His response was telling. He got frustrated, defensive, and said, "My mom has traveled the world because of my dad. Without him, she wouldn't have seen half the places she has."

In other words, the expectation of the man is to provide *money*, but not much else. In my mind, I thought, *I don't need a man to take me around the world. I can do that myself.*

What I needed was an actual relationship with the person I was married to.

I asked him if we could see a counselor. His friend, a therapist, came to our house to talk. In the middle of the conversation, when I expressed how much I wanted a deeper connection, Eric simply shut down. He got angry and was unable to tread those waters with me. After that session, he disappeared for a weekend, checked into a hotel, and relapsed. There was something broken inside of him that I was not suited to diagnose, let alone fix. While he coped via drugs, I lost hope day after day.

For months, this cycle repeated itself. He would disappear on a binge and I would go find him and bring him home. To make matters worse, I shouldered blame from his parents, who felt I was responsible because I rocked the boat. In their eyes, if I had just stayed quiet and gone along with things, everything would have been fine.

Eventually, I couldn't live the recurring nightmare any longer. I left and got my own apartment. I didn't file for divorce right away, but a few months later, he did—bringing an end to a marriage that, looking back, was doomed from the get-go.

The reality is: it's one thing to have a declaration of freedom; it's another thing to show a demonstration of fruit. It's easy to say, "I once was lost and now I'm found," but it's something else to show the long-term results of *being found*. In the soil we had been fed in, it seemed that as long as someone *said* they were transformed and walked out a clean life for a few months, they were good to go. After all, they had encountered the power of God—what more could they need?

I had no sense for inner healing, deep personal searching, and the time and intentionality required to walk in true personal stability and wholeness. As a result, I didn't ask the right questions, didn't have an eye for red flags, and jumped into a marriage that neither of us was suited to sustain.

Recently, I was talking to a colleague who said, "I gather that you're a very genuine person. You don't have time for people who aren't real."

How he surmised this, I'm not sure, but it was an accurate observation. Authenticity is not optional. I have very little time for facades or for people who say one thing and live another. It's not hard to see that much of this comes directly from growing up in a setting where speech didn't always align with reality. But even in my marriage, there was a clean surface with a broken subsurface that I did not discover until after the vows had been exchanged. The aftermath of a failed marriage made me even more attuned to when someone was *performing* instead of *being*. I naturally began to gravitate toward people who don't feel the need to put on a show—the ones who don't announce how great they are but whose lives quietly prove it.

And yet, I've also had to learn that not everyone who seems inauthentic is being malicious. Some people wear masks because they're afraid. Some put up walls because they simply don't know any other way to exist. And that's something I've softened toward over the years. If I encounter a lack of authenticity, I now ask myself, *Is this person just trying to protect themselves? Is there more beneath the surface?*

As time went on, I became more open to the concept of inner healing and a more holistic approach to mental and emotional well-being. Through my work in helping with job placement and teaching life skills, I began to feel anchored in the idea of helping people improve their lives.

At the time, I had no grand ministry vision, but as I plugged into new ministries and churches in Orange County, I was being primed for something more. I didn't know that before I could fully step into it, I'd have to unlearn one of my biggest struggles: the weight of toxic ownership. I would have to learn that there's a big difference between standing in spiritual authority and trying to *control* an outcome. I had a burden to help people, but God never intended for me to bear that alone. He simply asked me to pray, to fast, to intercede—but not to take on the responsibility of *fixing* it. That part was never mine to play. Whether I knew it or not, I was being tutored in the early building blocks of ministry and learning to drop my tendency toward over-responsibility.

As the 2000s passed, I stepped into a decade that would start with a barrage that I could have never predicted. Losing Justin was a precursor to a decade that would either break me or make me, or both. There would be tragedies I could not foresee and outcomes I could not control. If I was to frame up a life with Jesus where we co-labored to help others, I would have to survive the coming season. And if I was to survive, I would have to quickly learn to cast burdens at the feet of Jesus—or else be utterly crushed by them.

PART 2
Pruned for Purpose

CHAPTER FIVE

There's No Grid for Grief

"Grief can be a burden, but also an anchor." —Sarah Dressen

We dig internal wells that defy external chaos. This is life in the Kingdom of God. We know it's true that He who is *in us* is greater than he who is in the world (see 1 John 4:4), but if our eyes are on the world, this Scripture will feel as though it's been reversed. Our interior life as believers is our escape hatch and our refuge. Joy, peace, contentment—these are all inside jobs that don't arise from external sources.

Think of a submarine. They are able to withstand enormous amounts of pressure that would normally crush steel like a tin can. The reason they don't cave is because submarines are pressurized from the *inside*. The hull has its own pressure pushing back against the external force, creating equilibrium and safety for those inside.

So it goes with the Christian life.

We survive and thrive through enormous, crushing force by pressurizing ourselves from the inside out. Only in partnership with the Holy Spirit are we able to cultivate an interior atmosphere that trumps exterior mayhem.

There's no better example of this than the true story of the hymn we've all sung, "It Is Well with My Soul." These words are not some hollow, fake-it-'til-you-make-it phrase. Horatio Spafford wrote the hymn in 1873 in the midst of personal loss that few can understand. He was a devout Christian and a successful lawyer, but in 1871, the Great Chicago Fire devastated his finances. After a couple years of rebuilding, in 1873, he planned a trip to Europe with his wife and four daughters—where he would join his friend D.L. Moody, who was slated to preach in England. Due to last-minute business dealings, he sent his family ahead on the *SS Ville du Havre*, planning to join them later.

Along the way, the ship collided with another vessel and sank in the Atlantic. Spafford's wife, Anna, survived, but all four of their daughters, ages 12, 7, 4, and a year and a half, drowned. When his wife arrived in England, she sent Spafford a now-famous telegram: "Saved alone."

As Spafford traveled to reunite with his grieving wife, his ship passed the very spot where his daughters had passed not long before. It was there that he wrote the lyrics to "It Is Well with My Soul."

How can a man who has suffered the greatest losses imaginable confidently write, "You [Lord] have taught me to say, it is well with my soul"? The truth: he was living life from the inside out. Spafford was taught by God how to fix his mind on redemptive realities. This is not something that comes naturally to human beings, nor is it a gift you are suddenly given because you prayed a prayer of salvation. Living from the inside out is a learned, honed, and crafted lifestyle that comes at a price.

As I entered 2011, I was unaware of just how much the grace that was upon Horatio Spafford in the midst of tragedy would be required for my own survival. As a country, we were pulling out of the Recession, and young people were rethinking American economics. Wall Street was being occupied by activists, and extreme politics were being taken online as social media platforms were gaining steam. Ongoing wars in the Middle East were a point of division and the upcoming 2012 election was heated. Overall, the nation was in a season of unrest and upheaval, and though my career in workforce services was going well, I was also in a state of upheaval—at every level.

By God's grace, I was attending The Rock Church in Orange County under Pastor Jerry Dirmann at that time, and I really loved it. The church was stable, healthy, and I began my inner healing journey. It had been eight years since Justin's death. I had become somewhat settled on the matter, not because I had effectively dealt with it, but because I had pushed it aside.

The Rock had a program called Redeeming the Time—a six-week intensive that walked people through their past wounds and helped them heal. I didn't realize how much I needed it until I was in the middle of it, peeling back layers of pain I had buried for years. I also went through their Building Solid Lives discipleship program where they didn't just preach at you—they walked alongside you, helping you rebuild your life in a way that was sustainable. It is still one of the best Christian growth and discipleship programs I know, teaching believers to build their lives with God on the unshakeable foundation of the Word, in prayer, building a living relationship with God that leads to true transformation. As I grew through this ministry, the intense grief from losing Justin steadily passed, and the pangs that would come up through the years were becoming less and less unbearable. I had learned to value the time we *had* and not fixate on the time we *lost*. I was finding wholeness in areas I had long neglected, and life was finally looking up in a new way.

In the midst of this triumph, the first of three devastating dominoes fell in January of 2011 when I received an unexpected phone call. My ex-husband, Eric, was dead. During an extended drug binge, he took his own life while staying at his parents' house. Just a year before, Eric had called me, and we even met in person, making amends. We buried the past and left things between us on good terms. In response to this news, however, I was instantly face-to-face with a devastating two-headed monster called guilt and grief. Guilt reared powerfully, because I still felt responsible somehow. Despite the peace we had made between us before his passing, I had made myself emotionally responsible for someone I never could have saved. Although I knew that I had labored in vain trying to fix something that was never mine to fix, painful questions still haunted me. *Could I have changed the outcome? Is the weight of this on my shoulders?* While battling this monster on one hand, grief landed hard on the other side. I ached inside, realizing that the very life I once thought I would walk beside forever was now gone.

I spiraled emotionally. Inner healing and steps toward wholeness were finally being made in my life when this loss knocked me backward. It was like leaving the cancer ward in remission only to be hit in a head-on collision on the drive home. Pastor Randy and Ellie Collins offered to counsel me during that season, and I clung to those sessions like a lifeline. During our exchanges, I sensed a safety and a comfort that was otherwise absent in my day-to-day existence. But before I had even begun to fully process my state, another wave of grief crashed on the shores of my life.

By the end of that same year, my phone rang and I answered to the frantic and panicked voice of my mother. Through cries, tears, and pandemonium, she told me that my younger brother, Aaron, had shot himself in his room at their house. There was the disbelief and shock, which was quickly replaced by anguish and confusion. Sorrow upon sorrow was piling up in my soul quicker than I could alleviate the pain. Time collapses and expands in those seasons of sorrow. Certain moments in the night feel as if they last an eternity, while at the same time, weeks can pass in a blurry blink.

My brother Phillip, stationed in the Middle East at the time, flew home for the funeral. My sister Rachel, who had pursued medicine and was working as a doctor locally in

California and Margie and Priscilla flew in from Oklahoma. Each of us had taken different paths in life and career, but in that moment, all of those paths converged in devastating, unthinkable loss.

Shortly after the funeral, my parents moved to Oklahoma, throwing themselves into Pricilla and Margie's lives away from the coast, which now held such painful memories. Three months later, I got another call from my mom one morning. In a fairly calm voice, she said, "Byn killed himself last night."

Byn was my sister Priscilla's husband; they were in the middle of a divorce. They were both active-duty in the Air Force, where they had met. For a brief moment, I felt an odd sense of relief. *At least Priscilla is okay*, I thought. But then, as my mom kept talking, I realized something was off when she referred to Priscilla in the past tense.

"Wait...you said Byn killed himself. What about Priscilla?"

And then she said the words that shattered everything: "He killed Priscilla first."

I lost it. In fact, I lost *me*.

In some sense, I no longer had an individual identity but had become grief incarnate. I reeled and collapsed, traumatized afresh. For every waking moment of the day,

I had been existing in a blender of grief and pain. I had no framework for a string of tragedies like this—no one does. The tears, the panic, the shock, the anger, the confusion all spread out like tributaries in my soul. My eyes swam with tears as my heart raced, and I searched for words that wouldn't come. Then, my mom asked me to drive to Rachel's house to tell her what had happened.

I brought my dear friend, Steven McSweeney, with me for support, but it was still the hardest thing I had ever done. I leaned on Steven a lot, especially during Aaron's death. He and Pastor Paul were an anchor to our family during this horrific season.

When I broke it to Rachel, she simply couldn't process it. "No, no, this can't be happening," she repeated. None of us could process it. It felt like fiction—the end of a Shakespearean tragedy.

Over the next few hours, people started gathering at Rachel's house. Friends, family, my friends from The Rock, Pastor Paul and Cathy Bradshaw—everyone trying to make sense of something that made no sense at all. We had just buried Aaron and now Priscilla would need arrangements. It was too much loss, far too young, in too short a time. The media covered the incident extensively—military murder-suicides are always a massive story.

Once again, Phillip would be flown home from deployment to see yet another sibling laid to rest. We all gathered in Oklahoma to say our goodbyes. For several weeks, there remained an outflowing of love and support from those near the family. The presence of God doesn't always come with answers. Sometimes it just arrives in *people*. Numerous friends, leaders, and loved ones brought comfort while we mourned. During the fallout of everything, I remember sitting in Pastor Randy's office, barely able to breathe under the weight of it all, waiting for him to give me answers, to tell me *why* this was happening, to tell me *what* I was supposed to do now.

Instead, he just sat there for a long interval. As humble and genuine as a person can be, he said, "I don't know what to say right now, Sandi. I don't have an answer or words. I've never seen tragedy of this magnitude. I just want to sit with you in this."

He was okay not having answers? That was a turning point for me. Because for the first time, I realized that healing wasn't about finding or having all the right answers. It wasn't about someone fixing everything for me. It was about having someone *see* my pain, validate it, and sit with me in it. That moment gave me permission to just *be* in my grief, instead of feeling the urge to fix it or rush through recovery. This was much needed, because I had episodes where grief became so overwhelming that I didn't even know who I was mourning anymore. From Justin, to Eric, to Aaron, then Priscilla—I had lost so many people near me, at such a young age, that I could not identify which loss was the source of my sorrow from one day to the next.

Life felt surreal. When tragedy multiplies in a short period, your sense of normal becomes way off-kilter. You're being waterboarded by sorrow, and in the brief glimpses where oxygen is available, it doesn't feel like a relief but the bare minimum you need just to maintain a pulse. I was worn out by funerals, obituaries, flowers, receptions, and goodbyes.

Losing one person is devastating. Losing three in a year, in such gruesome fashion, is unimaginable. One way to define trauma is: too much, too fast. Our systems simply aren't able to process what's coming at us at the rate that it is. I was not sure how a person could survive so many losses so quickly—I just knew I had to.

* * *

There is no grid for grief. There is no roadmap, book, pamphlet, or step-by-step guide on how to wake up every morning when your entire world has been turned inside out.

There were times when I was asking, "Is it well with my soul?" far more than I was singing, "*It is* well with my soul."

You've probably heard it said that grief has stages—denial, anger, bargaining, depression, acceptance—but they don't always show up in a neat and tidy order. Grief is not linear. It avoids a straight line and can be unpredictable from one day to the next. You might suppose you're doing fine one day, and then a song, a smell, or a memory can hit you out of nowhere and bring you right back to the pain.

In the weeks after the losses, I discovered a grief system called SARAH, which represented the stages as Shock, Anger, Resentment, Acceptance, and Healing. When you are deep in the throes of pain, you just want a way out. However, this system helped me grasp that each stage serves a purpose, and our job is to embrace each one, rather than circumvent them.

Shock is actually a grace—helping you to function in those early days when everything is overwhelming. Your adrenaline spikes and life feels surreal—which is exactly what's required to survive those initial blows. Anger gives you the energy to process the injustice of loss. You may feel fired up, with a righteous indignation that motivates you to get out of bed in the morning. Resentment is often a way of assigning blame in order to make sense of it all. If left unchecked, it can be paralyzing, and roots of bitterness may set in. But if we process through it, we'll realize that placing blame on a person, circumstances, or God will not bring back our loved one, nor heal our hearts—which is exactly what leads us to *acceptance*. Acceptance is the threshold: you begin to let go of control, which is the bridge to actualizing your healing. Healing is what happens when you've walked through it all and allowed yourself to *feel it fully*. And this last step cannot be forgotten.

Grief demands to be felt. Pay now or pay later—grief comes back with interest when we delay the inevitable. I once met a woman who had been stuck in anger for forty years after her divorce. Her life had moved on, but her heart never did. And I have seen the same thing happen in my peer groups after the loss of a loved one. One person comes to mind who couldn't handle the weight of the pain of grief and numbed themselves with medication. For five years, they put their grief on pause. But when they finally came off the pills, it was as if they were right back standing over the casket—like time had never passed. Grief will patiently wait to be experienced, and we either go through it now or postpone the meeting for a later date. Meanwhile, life slips by. Meanwhile, our physical health may be impacted.

During that season, God in His mercy had already placed people in my life to walk through it with me. Despite going through the process of grief, I still remained a victim of my pain for a long, long time. By 2015, I was in a place of brokenness. Years of grief and loss had worn me down, leaving me feeling crushed, empty, and utterly worthless. I was stuck in a victim mindset, replaying the pain of my past like a broken record. I doubted that things would ever be *normal* again.

That season of my life was a rite of passage—a bridge from reacting to my past to reclaiming my identity. God kept presenting me with opportunities to heal. He was peeling back layers, validating my pain, and replacing the shame with truth. Eventually, The Rock paused their Wednesday night services to focus on home groups, so I started attending Dr. Michelle Corral's midweek gathering. The Rock was instrumental in discipling me in the Word and prayer daily, and I was ever so grateful for their inner healing program. I am still in touch with Pastor Kimberly and Jerry Dirmann today.

During that year, the Lord began prompting me to prepare for something unique regarding my future. Quickly, Dr. Michelle Corral became a spiritual mother to me, someone who modeled unconditional love. She taught me what it means to balance grace and truth. Dr. Corral's life matched her words. She lived the Bible, and I trusted her because I saw her consistency over time. In fact, that is the very formula for building trust: consistency + time.

I also formed a deep bond with Reverend Lou and Beverly Sheldon in those days. They became surrogate grandparents to me, offering caring hearts and quality time. We'd celebrate our shared June birthdays together in Palm Springs, and they always willingly answered my questions and offered rich insight. The connections between these mentors were nothing short of miraculous. When I mentioned to Dr. Corral that I'd been spending time with Lou and Beverly, she exclaimed, "Wait a minute—you know Lou and Beverly Sheldon? They were my mentors at Melodyland School of Theology!"

Here I was, being mentored by people who had shaped each other decades earlier. These relationships were a lifeline, and I was quickly discovering that God was placing me in an intentional network where my healing and growth could prosper over time.

A pivotal moment came that year when God sent a man named Tim Bagwell into my life. The day he showed up at our church in Orange County, I had been taking steps toward inner healing and wholeness, but could not find a legitimate breakthrough from the victim spirit that ruled my thoughts. I noticed right away that he ministered with both an authority and a sensitivity that pierced my heart.

As his message came to a close, he called me out of the congregation and asked me to come forward. He didn't know me from anyone—it was his first time in that pulpit. Yet he opened his mouth and God spoke through him: "You've been broken and crushed. Nobody in this room knows the depth of crushing you've been through, but God has seen it all." He had a fatherly way about him, deeply validating the pain which I had been through. He continued: "You have been brought so low, literally to a place of feeling valueless. The only thing I can liken this to is the story of Humpty Dumpty." He then began to recite the Humpty Dumpty nursery rhyme. "I know that's not spiritual, but it's the picture God's giving me," he said.

Yet it was *so* true.

"All the king's horses and all the king's men couldn't put him back together again." This was a genuine validation from a man of God who represented the Father God to me.

And then he said something that wrecked me in an irreversible way: "You've been stuck, but today God is breaking you free from the victim spirit. I don't know you, and today is the first day I've met your pastor, but today you're receiving her mantle."

It meant more than I'm able to articulate on a page, but it changed the trajectory of my thoughts and feelings from focusing on my pain to seeing myself as a victor who had overcome. As his hand rested on my head and he prayed, the weight of God's glory fell on me.

As the power of God hit me, I began weeping uncontrollably. My knees buckled and I fell to the floor. Years of grief poured out all at once, but in the best way possible. For the first time, I felt seen—and my excruciating pain had been fully validated. When I went home that night, the weeping didn't stop. It wasn't the kind of crying that leaves you drained and hopeless. It was a cleansing—a washing away of the years of pain I had carried. The power of God set me free. I knew that something had shifted—God was preparing me for something new, something more. I was moving from victim to victor.

When it came to feeling like a victim, I realized I had a choice in the matter. I could stay stuck in it, or I could allow my pain to be transformed into something meaningful. That didn't mean forgetting or speeding through the process. It didn't mean minimizing the losses I had suffered. It meant letting them shape me in a way that would allow me to help others. It meant using my story to remind people that there *is* a way through. The pain doesn't have to define you—it can *refine* you.

For most of my life, I lived with a mask. I didn't express outward emotions; I kept my real thoughts and feelings locked away, and I projected to the world what I *wanted* them to see—not what was necessarily true beneath the surface. All this was changing now.

I started to let my guard down.

I started to let myself be seen.

I started to heal.

The glorious process of healing wasn't just about feeling better—it was about learning to live again. I was no longer just surviving the intense, paralyzing pangs of grief; I was allowing God to transform me through it. Where I had once coped and numbed my way through pain, I was now submitting to the process of heaven in the midst of it. The pain didn't disappear overnight, but it no longer owned me. I was exiting the most heart-wrenching and chaotic season of my life and simultaneously was on my way to a stability that I had never known. The grief that had burdened me was beginning to anchor me—not in sorrow, but in my Savior. In time, the words of that old hymn would become my own:

HERE COMES JOY

Though Satan should buffet, though trials should come
Let this blest assurance control
That Christ has regarded my helpless estate
And hath shed His own blood for my soul
It is well with my soul

CHAPTER SIX
Layers of Healing

"Sweetly broken, wholly surrendered." —Vineyard Worship

In life, change is inevitable; growth is *optional*. However, those who commit to walking in the Kingdom of God will find that life is reminiscent of a greenhouse—an environment where growth is not only possible but *inevitable*. No matter how harsh the conditions outside, the greenhouse gives warmth, water, and shelter. It protects tender sprouts from the scorching sun, shields fragile leaves from violent winds, and ensures that what is planted has the best possible shot at thriving.

Healing happens in much the same way. It doesn't happen while simultaneously being under constant attack. It happens in an environment where the conditions are intentionally cultivated for growth. For years, I had tried to heal in survival mode, expecting to flourish while still exposed to the same toxic patterns and lies that had kept me bound. But real healing required a shift—it meant residing in the greenhouse of God's presence, where the soil was rich, the light was steady, and the Gardener Himself was invested in my restoration.

As you would expect from any plant, growth didn't happen in a hurry. There were layers to the process—seasons of pruning, seasons of stretching toward the light, and even periods when it seemed like nothing was happening at all. But in the safety of God's presence, something was always at work beneath the surface—and still is. Healing wasn't just about repairing what had been broken; it was about becoming something new altogether.

We all know the hymn "Amazing Grace," which announces, "I once was lost and now I'm found." But what happens once you're found? What occurs when you've been located by the plan of heaven? For me, the process of inner healing was not just the *next step* in my walk with Jesus, but the *necessary* step if I was to continue ahead. In the church world, we tend to compartmentalize discipleship, viewing it merely as Bible study, knowledge acquisition, or developing better prayer habits. In reality, deliverance and inner healing are not processes that precede discipleship but they *are* discipleship.

My journey through grief and being healed of trauma was not something that needed to happen in order for me to grow in God but it was the very essence of growing in God. You might be tempted to think that inner healing is a special deliverance-focused Seal Team 6 operation reserved for those who've been through the worst of the worst. But countless interactions and testimonies later, I have found that even those who've lived relatively calm, "normal" lives often have great need of inner healing and wholeness. Why? Because it's not just the enormous wounds or deep cuts that can put a life at risk. It's the little cuts, grown infected, that can do just as much damage over time.

One of the things I love about sharing my story is that it does not follow the typical Christian testimony formula, where everything is bad, then at one turning point everything changes, and then life is glorious in God. In fact, I would argue that *most* testimonies are actually not structured this way. The best testimonies, though, are the ones where people vulnerably submit to the healing process of God and remain faithful through the years.

No one wakes up one day and suddenly has no issues. It takes time, layers, and a willingness to face the hard things. Through this process, I've learned that you don't have to be perfect to be loved. You don't have to *arrive* at some arbitrary destination to be valued by God. He works with you as you go—building the plane while you're flying it. For the longest time, I thought healing was a one-and-done process. You face a wound, you bandage it, and you move on. But I've come to see it differently now. Healing is a *lifetime* journey. It's a daily choice to let God work in me, wound by wound, layer by layer.

This does *not* mean that you are bound to your trauma from here on out. God has not doomed you to a life of addressing your constant pain like a cruel game of Whac-A-Mole. Make no mistake there is absolute *freedom* available in Christ. What it *does* mean is that as we roll up our sleeves and become the best version of ourselves we can be, we will inevitably find old wounds and issues that need some loving care. Think of it as cleaning a castle. You may have 90 percent of the place spotless, but over time, you will enter rooms that have long been ignored and will have to do some maintenance to get it looking its best. Don't be discouraged! God has calculated all of these variables into the glorious life that He has for you.

As I shifted out of severe grief and trauma and into a process of healing, I had to learn that I was exactly where I needed to be at any given time in the process. It's not uncommon to hear someone in church say, "I'm not where I was, but I'm not where I need to be." But I would ask, *how do you know you are not where you need to be?* Just because you haven't *arrived* does not mean you are out of joint. If someone is in an ambulance being taken to the hospital after an accident, they might think, "I'm not where I need to be," because they are not safely at home enjoying their evening. But the truth is, in the grand scheme of things, the back of the ambulance is *exactly* where they need to be. It's not where they'll stay, but for healing to have its way, this is where you must be plotted on the timeline of life at this given moment. For example, we would never condemn a newborn for nursing just because in the future they will move past nursing. We don't judge them based on where they will be one day but we evaluate them for what they need *right now*. For me, my needs were great in the months and years that followed my season of loss.

I knew I would not find peace on an island. As my healing journey unfolded, I noticed a common theme:

every step, breakthrough, and milestone happened in the context of community. I gleaned and grew from resources and relationships with mentors such as Dr. Corral, Debby Temmer, Pastors Kimberly and Jerry Dirmann, and others whom we will discuss in chapters to come. Relationships house our futures. Even today, when a person comes to me for inner healing, my first question is always: who is your community? Because the truth is, healing doesn't happen in isolation. If wounds were created in relationship, healing must also come through relationship.

One of the most dangerous things I've witnessed—both in my own life and in the lives of those I've tried to help—is the refusal to be accountable to a community or covering. The people who remain trapped in cycles of dysfunction, addiction, or spiritual bondage are often the same people who refuse to let anyone speak truth into their lives. They don't allow themselves to be corrected. They isolate themselves from voices that might challenge them, and as a result, they become blind to their own destruction. That's where the concept of the Johari Window comes in. While being mentored by Debby Temmer, I learned this powerful heuristic. It's a psychological framework that breaks our self-awareness into four quadrants:

1. What we know about ourselves that others also see
2. What others see about us that we don't see about ourselves
3. What we project about ourselves that isn't actually true
4. What neither we nor others see, but that only God can reveal

The most dangerous quadrant is the second one—the things about ourselves that *other people can see*, but we *can't*. If we are not open to hearing from those who love us, we stay blind. In that state, we don't even register when we're headed for disaster. I've sat across from people who were spiraling, trying to warn them, and watched them dig their heels in deeper. It's easy to see things in others once we've overcome them. We can get defensive, make excuses, shift blame, or retreat into a victim mentality. And the tragedy is that we can go on *believing* these lies when we're lacking accountability. We might think we've done the work, we've already healed, and we don't need to change. But those watching from the outside can see all the signs clearly.

It's why I tell people all the time: You need safe people in your life. You need people you trust, people who will tell you the truth, even when you don't want to hear it. The enemy does his business best in isolation. When you don't have anyone to challenge your perspective, you start believing your own deception, which is exactly how people stay stuck for years—sometimes decades or even a lifetime. But if we can embrace the discomfort of accountability, if we can invite trusted people to help us see what we can't see, healing can happen in an expedited fashion. To pull this off, people need a safe, authentic community where they can be vulnerable, where they won't be met with unfair judgment or rejection.

These safe harbors facilitate what is perhaps the most important starting ingredient for healing: *vulnerability*. If therapy is a train, vulnerability is the track that it rides upon. For much of my life, I couldn't afford to be vulnerable. It was a dangerous game, opening yourself to attack or dismissal. Showing your weakness to an unsafe person leads to destruction. However, showing your weakness to God leads to edification.

As sessions came and went and I began to mend, I saw that vulnerability welcomed healing salve to any area of my soul that was willing to display it. I became eager to discuss and unpack the broken parts of myself. Sometimes trials don't create weaknesses, but expose them. When this exposure happens, we have the chance to vulnerably own them head-on. James wrote, *"My brethren, count it all joy when you fall into various trials, knowing that the testing of your faith produces patience. But let patience have its perfect work, that you may be perfect and complete, lacking nothing"* (James 1:2–4).

Being perfect, mature, complete, with no lack sounds like a wonderful state—but we don't get there by dodging the exposure of our weaknesses. We get there by counting those vulnerabilities as a *joy* to navigate. One of the more common hindrances to vulnerability is pride. Pride hides what vulnerability admits. Appearances and perceptions dominated my thinking for far too long, and I carried a pride into adulthood that did *not* want to admit weakness.

God began to nudge me—sometimes gently, sometimes not—into places where I had to be vulnerable. At first, I resisted with everything in me, desperate to not look foolish. I didn't want to ruin my reputation. I wanted to protect myself but God is more interested in our transformation than He is our self-preservation.

I'll never forget one of the first times I felt God asking me to step out in vulnerability during that season. I was in church during worship and I felt Him so clearly say, "Get down on your knees." I looked around the room—no one else was kneeling. The thought of being the only one, of drawing that kind of attention, terrified me. I wrestled with it, and I didn't do it that day, and left feeling ashamed of my own dignity. But the next time He asked, I did—and something broke inside me.

It was the beginning of a journey where I devalued the perceptions of others and properly appraised the approval of God. Over time, I began to see that vulnerability was less about weakness and more about surrender. The control I had maintained over my life was being released to God, and as it was, everything began to flourish.

* * *

To get better, I had to choose to not only see my wounds, but my worth. Reconnecting with God was easy. Reconnecting with myself was a process. Paul wrote, *"Now all things are of God, who has reconciled us to Himself through Jesus Christ, and has given us the ministry of reconciliation"* (2 Corinthians 5:18). This area of Scripture is the only time that specific word Greek word "reconciled" (καταλλαγῆς) is used in the New Testament. The full definition bears exploring. It doesn't just mean "brought back together" or "reconnected." It literally means "restored to favor."

As Christians, we understand that God has reconciled us to Himself. But what about this "ministry" of reconciliation? We generally take this to mean that we are now tasked with helping others be reconciled to God as well, which is true. However, I want to propose that within our ministry of reconciliation, we are to be reconciled to our true selves as well. We are to be brought into *restored favor* with our own selves.

My healing was not just about addressing the trauma I'd been through. It was also about learning to be *present* with myself again. There were times when I was so out of touch with my own needs that I'd be standing in freezing rain without even noticing. Discomfort, an umbrella, or finding shelter had not so much as registered in my brain. Ultimately, I had forgotten how to care for myself. Severe trauma disconnects you from everything—even your own body, emotions, and true self. As I mentioned earlier, trauma is *too much, too fast,* and can lead to neglect, which is *too little, too late.*

For people with chronic trauma, *dissociation* can become a way of life (more accurately said: a way of death). Studies show that individuals with complex PTSD (C-PTSD) often develop a pattern of emotional numbing or "checking out" from their own experiences. This detachment is the brain's way of protecting itself from pain, but over time, it creates a deep disconnect from self-awareness, basic needs, and personal identity.

It's important to note reconciliation to yourself is not some humanist, man-centered, self-promoting doctrine. We see the need for this playing out in Scripture over and over. Jesus routinely met people's physical, emotional, and spiritual needs by engaging their own assessment before acting. He asked the blind man in Mark 10:51, *"What do you want me to do for you?"*—not because He didn't know, but because self-awareness is an essential part of healing. The very act of prayer itself both engages God and calls on our ability to properly self-evaluate.

This pattern of restoration has been at play since the beginning. After Adam and Eve had sinned, they found themselves in isolation, hiding from the very One who gave them life. God made an inquiry asking, "Adam, where are you?" We can be certain that God knew exactly where Adam was. The reason for the question was that God wanted *Adam* to know where Adam was.

Think of the prodigal son. He was living on a diet of pig slop—completely broke and disconnected from himself and reality. What happened just before he got the bright idea to return to the father? The Bible says, *"he came to himself"* (see Luke 15:17).

I, too, had to *come to myself*. Where I had once been uncomfortable with mirrors, antsy in a room alone, and disconnected from the true me, I started to notice my needs, name my feelings, and embrace the beautiful pain and joy of existence in any given breath of time. I went from a stranger to myself to a friend to myself, looking after my own welfare. I checked my spiritual boxes with extended time in the Word, developing a fiery prayer life, and daily declaring truth over myself. I was no longer neglecting my own state—I engaged in self-care routines, eating well, and prioritizing sound sleep.

God was not just interested in changing my mental state. He was invested in pioneering new pathways in my soul, new routines in my day, and rectifying habits that would set me up to run this race for the long haul.

There's a tendency in some circles to expect instant results—whether it's deliverance, a miraculous healing, or a snap-of-the-finger transformation. And while I absolutely believe in the power of God to bring sudden breakthroughs, I've also seen the beauty of healing as a process. The long, slow work of grace and truth over time can lead to lasting freedom. Had God burst onto the scene in 2012 and instantly waved away all pain and trauma in a blink—I would have been deprived of the learning, the insight, the self-discovery, the strength, and the beauty of a deep, detailed restoration. I would not have learned what makes me tick, what caused certain reactions, and I certainly would not have gained the tools needed to help others in their hour of darkness.

When I think about the work God has called me to do—whether it's through inner healing, prayer ministry, or just walking alongside someone in their journey—I see it as a blend of grace, truth, and time. These three elements are the foundation of everything I've learned and the way I approach helping others. With this trifecta, complete turnarounds are possible. It's not always about a quick fix in the prayer line at the altar. It's about a consistent commitment to knowing God, knowing ourselves, and yielding at every turn.

The truth is, there are mass numbers of people who sit in the church pews for years learning a thing or two about God while never once learning a thing about themselves. They cannot name their needs, which steals their healing, and they cannot name their gifts, which steals their influence. Solomon wrote, *"The purposes of a person's heart are deep waters, but one who has insight draws them out"* (Proverbs 20:5 NIV). We need insight to look deep into our own hearts to find what is there: good, bad, or ugly.

Losing three people close to me in such a short span forced me to look deep. Not only that, but at a certain point, it occurred to me that over a decade had passed since Justin's death and I still had not properly grieved him. I simply buried my memory of him and his death. I wouldn't speak of him. The circumstances surrounding what happened were such a sensitive and painful topic for me that I simply did not engage it.

During one particular stretch, the Lord prompted me to slow down and refrain from traveling for a spell. He drew me into His presence in the most gentle way. The Holy Spirit began showing a replay of myself. He shined and showed me that I had carried such shame toward Justin's death. I had not allowed myself to feel—and the weight of the grief had been on my shoulders for far too long. He was so gentle, yet displayed the truth. It was like shining a flashlight in the dark.

Coming face to face with truth with a prompting of permission to grieve I sat and wept for half an hour. The crying turned to sobbing and then wailing. I emptied an entire tissue box grieving Justin that night. Grief had been stuck, lodged in my soul—and I imagine it had come out in other ways—body and mind. During the grieving process, the crying became so fierce I said, "Lord, I can't breathe anymore." While it hurt physically, the release was so needed and peace-infusing. I grieved years and years and years of loss in a single evening. Seventeen years in total—the number of redemption. In some ways, I'm still grieving them all—but it's more so the itch of a scar rather than the pain of an open wound.

The more I learn about healing, the more I realize this: our hearts were never designed for brokenness. Mankind was created before the fall and because of that, our hearts were made to believe in *finality*—finality in love, in security, in belonging. We were wired for complete trust. Before sin entered the world, we were meant to fully trust in God's goodness without question or doubt. But when sin entered, so did false beliefs. Suddenly, instead of knowing we are fully loved, we believe we are permanently abandoned. Instead of standing firm in our worth, we shrink back in shame. And shame is one of the most sinister and destructive forces in the world. It distorts our identity. It doesn't just make us feel bad about something we've done—it convinces us that something is wrong with who we are. And when we believe that lie, we hide. We hide our pain, our questions, our need for connection. We build walls to keep rejection out, but in doing so, we keep healing out as well.

Shame told me I was illegitimate. Being born out of wedlock meant I was unwanted, not supposed to be here, an accident. But God says that the circumstances of our birth don't determine our worth. I unlearned subtle beliefs and tore down strongholds in my perceptions, embracing the reality spoken in Jeremiah: *"Before I formed you in the womb I knew you; before you were born I sanctified you; I ordained you a prophet to the nations"* (Jeremiah 1:5 NKJV).

I've learned over the years that sometimes, the very instincts you want to act on are the ones you need to challenge. I've learned that when I feel the urge to draw the sword, that's often the moment to sheath it. I identified with Peter stepping out to defend Jesus before His arrest—feeling as though I was doing a service, but in fact, I was acting out of a sense of competition or my own sense of justice.

As several years passed from my season of brokenness, I did much learning, unlearning, and relearning. I reclaimed what was stolen and no longer neglected the hidden parts of myself. For so long, the very systems God created in me to hold onto truth had been hijacked to hold onto my pain. Healing was not just a process of moving forward, but a process of retrieving something I was always meant to have—wholeness, trust, and a shame-free existence. Day by day, my destiny was coming together. I had much to discover, much to share, much to mend, but I was on my way.

CHAPTER SEVEN
A New Garment

"God has given us two hands, one to receive with and the other to give with." —Billy Graham

A mantle is more than a piece of fabric in Bible stories. In the Old Testament, it was a sign of authority, calling, and divine empowerment. Prophets and priests wore them as a mark of their office. Elijah passed his to Elisha, signifying a double portion of his prophetic grace. When you received a mantle, it meant God was commissioning you for something greater. Mantles are never given without a mandate.

When Tim Bagwell prophesied, "You've been broken and crushed. You've been stuck," I knew exactly what he meant. But the little note at the tail end of the prophecy, that I was receiving a "new mantle," left me with questions. Not bad questions, but a healthy inquiry into what that meant and where God was sending me. What did it mean to carry the anointing that Dr. Corral was carrying? I knew that assignments, territories, and mountains of influence were in my future, but the details I had yet to piece together.

Pastor Bagwell was not speaking in vague encouragement—he was declaring a heavenly change where the tectonic plates of my spirit were shifting. I was undergoing a spiritual upgrade and taking on new levels of responsibility, anointing and authority. In this, I would gradually shift from being in dire need *of* ministry to meeting dire needs *through* my ministry.

Here's the thing about mantles: **they come at a cost.** When Elisha took up Elijah's mantle, he didn't just inherit power—he inherited responsibility. He stepped into something bigger than himself, something that would stretch and refine him. Most people will never understand the price that Dr. Corral has paid to carry the glory of God in her ministry. She spends countless hours in prayer, hours in the Word every day, sacrificing many other things she could be doing to promote herself and her ministry. She does not defend herself when an attack comes; she lives a life dead to self and surrendered to Jesus Christ. On television, people see this lovely woman speaking on a stage or praying with such power from God. This may look glamorous to some, yet we may never take into account the surrender and price she's paid. A mantle isn't about status; it's about serving God's people with a greater capacity. It's about carrying His presence into places where it's needed most. In order to do that successfully, we must be dead to self.

While keynote speaking at glory-filled conferences has its place, I knew part of my calling was to walk alongside people in the trenches of life—often away from the public eye.

This became especially clear when a pastor I had known from California connected me with a woman in desperate need. At the time, I was professionally running workforce service programs and, in the past, through petitioning Dr. Corral's ministry helped a single mother who was living in a shelter purchase a car. Dr. Corral not only made the purchase possible—she went above and beyond, providing the young mom of three with a vehicle far nicer than she would have ever requested for herself.

As a result of God showing up for people in desperate need, this pastor from California would send people in difficult circumstances my way for help. This precious pastor sat down and described a 30-year-old woman named Bella, trapped in a situation that could only be described as a physical, emotional, and spiritual *Egypt*.

She lived in her father's house, where abuse of every kind had become her daily reality. Beaten, violated, and unable to break free, Bella was paralyzed by fear. Her father's violence had fractured her spirit. She had tried to leave before, only to be hunted down, dragged back, and brutalized for daring to escape.

She drove two hours weekly to Orange County, showing up at church with visible bruises and black eyes. When I first heard about her situation, I knew this wasn't just about helping her find a job. This was about her need to break out of absolute bondage. It was about an *exodus*.

I first met Bella for a meal to start building a relationship. I picked her up on my lunch break, and I had one goal: to love. In that particular setting, at that particular time, love meant not pressing her with questions, not asking about the bruises or the situation but just letting her share as she felt comfortable. As we drove, the Holy Spirit spoke quietly to me: *She's pregnant.* I kept the thought to myself, knowing it wasn't the time or place to say anything.

A NEW GARMENT

Over the next two months, I continued to simply build trust with Bella, taking her for meals and letting her share without pressure or obligation, taking her to Dr. Corral's church with me whenever possible. It was always difficult to conceal the black eyes and facial bruises, especially since a new one seemed to appear every week courtesy of her father. When I asked her about them, she would simply say, "I got in trouble." Witnessing this every week left me consumed with anger, often wanting to go to her home, armed, to confront her father. Nevertheless, I stayed patient and persistent, wanting to keep a completely open door for Bella.

One day at lunch, she finally confided in me that she was pregnant—by her father—and wanted an abortion. She had to make a decision soon because, during that time, there was a gestational limit prohibiting abortion after so many months. The circumstances of her pregnancy were truly horrific, and hearing her verbalize it was brutal. This was a decision no human being should ever have to make. How could I tell her what to do? It was enough of a struggle for me to control my emotions and be a good witness to Bella. I have never wanted to kill anyone until now.

I've developed a custom through the years to listen inwardly to the gentle leadings of the Spirit. When I don't know what to say, He is not short on words. Jesus said, *"Do not worry about how or what you should answer, or what you should say. For the Holy Spirit will teach you in that very hour what you ought to say"* (Luke 12:11–12 NKJV).

As we sat in the silence that followed Bella's news, I felt the Holy Spirit nudge me: *Don't tell her what to do. Lead her to Me.*

So, sitting across from her, I said, "Bella, I can't tell you what to do. But I can help you pray and ask God what He wants."

We bowed our heads, and I prayed the simplest prayer I could muster: "Lord, Your Word says if anyone lacks wisdom, we can ask You for it. So, we're asking: what does Bella do in this situation?"

Two things happened. First, Bella's trust deepened that day. She didn't feel pressured, judged, or like she was fed a rehearsed dogmatic speech. Second, she was now positioned to receive the wisdom of heaven. After we finished our meal, we headed to service at Dr. Corral's church as planned.

As usual, we sat quietly in the back to avoid drawing attention to Bella's fresh bruises and other visible signs of trauma. As hard as we tried to not draw attention, we must have been the elephant in the room, even though Bella hid her pregnancy effectively. Seeing the bruises on Bella's face in a past service, Dr. Corral had asked what she could do to help. After I explained that Bella needed a miracle from God, without revealing her pregnancy or any other personal details, Dr. Corral wrote Bella's name down and put it in her Bible for daily prayer. She then asked me to please keep her abreast of *anything at all* that Bella might need.

As Dr. Corral began her sermon on that day, she announced she would be speaking about *the womb*—and what God has placed in our spiritual wombs. Shocked but not shocked, I knew that our prayer from just a few hours prior was on the brink of being answered.

Dr. Corral declared, "What God has placed in your womb, He has given life to. It is His will for this to live. You will not abort what God has given you."

Of course, she knew nothing of the personal circumstances going on in Bella's life. I glanced at her out of the corner of my eye and saw a face mixed with shock and awe. She was hearing God speak directly to her situation.

As the service came to a close, Dr. Corral began to flow in the prophetic and give individual words to people. At the end, she added, "There is someone here—yes, you know who you are. God is saying that a baby was saved from an abortion because of this message today."

Bella broke down. The weight of God's love, His clear voice speaking to her, shattered every doubt. I remained quiet, letting her experience God and His leading without interruption or commentary.

On the way home, she looked at me and said, "That was God. I know what to do now." She then explained to me that as Dr. Corral was prophesying to individuals, Bella asked God to give her a prophetic word but to not have Dr. Corral approach her. The shame was too great. In His immeasurable kindness, God met Bella that night, right where she was and right where she needed to be met.

Within a week, Bella called me.

"I'm packing my car," she said. "My dad's at work, and I'm leaving. I'm driving to my sister's in Texas." I was elated beyond my ability to express. Bella had been through hell on earth yet she didn't give up. God hand-selected a tribe of intercessors and pastors that aren't named here to break her out of a devastation that has taken the lives of many women, including my own sister. This day the kingdom of God was triumphant. Jesus Himself won this battle for Bella. The exodus was fully underway. She was leaving emotional and physical Egypt, more than five months pregnant.

By God's grace, she made it to Texas safely, where her sister gave her a safe place to stay. In the weeks that followed, she began preparing for the next chapter. One Sunday, she called me asking for prayer. Her voice sounded quieter than usual, and there was a sadness in her tone.

"I went to an adoption agency today," she said.

By then, about six months along, she knew she was carrying a boy. It took every ounce of strength for her to make the decision to place him for adoption. She then asked me to pray for her, as it was an incredibly difficult decision.

I began to pray as she listened silently. Then, in the midst of the prayer, I felt the Lord speak: "I am with your son. I have called him Jeremiah, a prophet to the nations. My hand is on him, and I will guide his steps."

At that moment, Bella started crying uncontrollably. There was a long silence on the line as my mind raced, trying to understand what she was going through. Finally, she whispered, "I didn't tell you. I didn't tell you..."

"What didn't you tell me?"

She replied, "When I was at the agency, they gave me a big binder to fill out information about him. They also asked if I wanted to name him, and I said, 'Yes, I named him Jeremiah.'" Through tears she added, "This is confirmation. God has His hand on him."

A few months later, after displaying so much courage, Bella gave birth to a healthy baby boy. Naming him

Jeremiah gave a sense of sealing God's promise over his life wherever he may go. The decision to place him for adoption was heartbreaking, but it was also a step of faith—and one she took with joy—knowing she was giving him a chance at the life God intended for him.

Today, Bella is a leader at her church and dreams of providing specialized therapy for others who've been through trauma on such a level. She has even started the fundraising process for the ministry, and God has shown up mightily. Though she understandably still must navigate some of the fallout from her past, she is surrounded by a loving community and continues to grow in the grace of God.

Walking with Bella during her darkest hour was a "Coming to Jesus" moment on how God feels about the preservation of life. Through this experience, God taught me His heart for life. Before meeting her, I knew in my mind that God was pro-life and valued each and every baby—born and unborn. Yet I had not fully grasped just how far He will go to provide the means and the grace to choose life and allow the ordained purpose of the child to flourish, even in the most difficult of circumstances. It was a firsthand encounter with His love and intervention.

Sometimes, God doesn't just want you to read about His heart. He wants you to *experience* it. And with Bella, I felt like I was in the very chambers of God's heart, seeing His pulse as life unfolded.

* * *

God calls us to help others, but not prematurely. In the same way that a baby needs to come to full term in order to have the best chance at survival and success, the plan of heaven must come full term. When I walked alongside Bella during her pregnancy, I wanted to step in and fix everything right away. I wanted to mother her, protect her, and make the decisions for her. When she faced a crossroad, my early instincts would have been to give her my own beliefs, insights, and biblical rationale. But God tapped me on the shoulder and slowed me down, time after time. He reminded me that my role wasn't actually to rescue her at all, but to trust Him to lead her personally.

If I had intervened, I might have robbed her of the powerful encounter she had at Dr. Corral's church. I might have taken away her opportunity to hear directly from God and experience His plan unfolding in her life. If we are constantly trying to speak on behalf of God to people, we make no room for people to hear from God directly. We are playing telephone while God wants a face-to-face interaction.

Growth happens in the struggle, in the digging, the waiting, the piecing together. It's where trust is built, and where we learn to hear God's voice for ourselves. Far too often, Christians want to become the bridge to God. We extend ourselves from one edge of the cliff to the other, telling those we mentor exactly where to walk and what to do. But the Gospel declares that we, as human beings, are not the bridge to God. Jesus Himself is the bridge to God, so if we can get people to Him, He takes the reins. Does this mean that we don't advise, counsel, prophesy, and teach? Of course not. But what it *does* mean is that in moments where someone is making a critical decision, don't prematurely rob them of their chance to hear from God and make the call.

This is the model of Jesus. During His recorded life and ministry, He asked a total of 307 questions. Meanwhile, He Himself is asked a total of 183. Consider it: Jesus asked more questions than He even answered. Why? Because God knows that gentle curiosity will lead people to discover the conclusions that He has already deposited in them. Discipleship is less about dogmatic lectures and more about gentle leading.

Over time, I began to notice that *joy* was the hallmark of authentic ministry. Whether it was Bella or someone else walking beside someone else, the eruption of joy was a consistent byproduct of healing. In fact, joy was not just the result of healing, but part of the very process of healing. I would sit with women through inner healing sessions and noted that a weight of grief would come as trauma was addressed. The person was finally confronting the truth of the pain. But once it was dealt with, a release of joy would follow—giving evidence to their newfound freedom.

The Greek word *charis*, meaning "grace," appears 156 times in the New Testament—which is clear proof of its foundational role in the Christian life. Closely related is the word *chara*, meaning "joy." This is not a fleeting emotion, but a deep, enduring sense of well-being rooted in a relationship with God.

This connection is clear: grace births joy. When we truly grasp God's unearned favor toward us, joy naturally flows. Grace lifts the burden of striving, heals shame, and invites us into a life of spiritual delight regardless of our circumstances.

Jesus Himself prayed that his followers would experience full joy. Why? Because He knew that in Him, the fullness of grace had come—and with it, the promise of lasting joy.

One of the most transformative turning points in my journey followed this exact pattern. It came during my 30s as I sat in a meeting in Washington, D.C. Up until then, I didn't have the language—or the permission—to name my experiences for what they were. I had processed the pain of childhood and the trauma I had navigated as an adult. However, I had not put my finger fully on the issue.

That changed in a prophetic meeting with a minister named Sharon Stone. A small group of us were gathered in our nation's capital. I'll never forget her walking up to me, looking into my eyes, and saying, "Nobody knows what you've been through to get here. God says, 'I've rescued you from abuse.'"

That word—*abuse*—landed like a lightning bolt in my spirit. I had never even let myself use the phrase. It was the first time a person representing authority from God named it. Growing up, my reality had been dismissed so often that I'd learned to do the same to myself. My family lived in denial, valuing appearances over truth. Speaking out meant you'd pay the price. Admitting that I had been abused meant breaking the unspoken rule of silence among so many families.

But in that moment, God validated my experience. That validation broke something in me—not in a bad way, but like a dam bursting. It lifted a veil of shame I didn't even realize I was carrying. Later, in private, I wept and processed it with God. And, per usual, what replaced the trauma was a newfound measure of *joy*.

Joy isn't just laughter. It's more than a smile. Transcending happiness or short bursts of serotonin, joy finds its source in God's interaction with our hearts. It's a profound, supernatural *bubbling up* that transforms lives. Solomon understood this reality thousands of years ago when he wrote, *"A joyful heart helps healing"* (Proverbs 17:22 CEB).

This isn't just a biblical reality, but is born out by science as well. One of the more fascinating things I learned is how the heart and brain work together to store and process emotions. As I grew in my understanding of these things, God led me to research the HeartMath Institute, an organization that studies neurocardiology—the connection between the heart and the brain. Their findings have been astonishing. The heart sends more signals to the brain than the brain sends to the heart, which was a complete surprise. Our hearts actually learn, remember, and influence the way our entire body functions.

This is why trauma runs so deep. Our bodies store experiences, especially painful ones, and without healing, those experiences shape the way we move through the world. This is why trauma, even trauma we have forgotten, can cause destructive behaviors and patterns in our lives. In his famous book *The Body Keeps the Score,* van der Kolk writes, "We have learned that trauma is not just an event that took place sometime in the past; it is also the imprint left by that experience on mind, brain, and body. This imprint has ongoing consequences for how the human organism manages to survive in the present. Trauma results in a fundamental reorganization of the way the mind and brain manage perceptions. It changes not only how we think and what we think about, but also our very capacity to think."[1]

This is exactly why certain triggers can send us spiraling without even realizing it—because the subconscious mind holds onto pain long after our conscious mind has forgotten it. Just like my hazy trips to Arkansas as a child or the trauma that occurred in my own neighborhood, I personally had held onto pain that my conscious mind had forgotten. These things limited me in areas because I found myself growing up but not growing *within*. If growth in a person stalls out, it could be the result of unprocessed pain. For instance, I remember sitting with a young woman recently, watching as a fragmented part of

---

1. van der Kolk, Bessel, M.D. . *The Body Keeps the Score: Brain, Mind, and Body in the Healing of Trauma.* (New York: Viking 2014).

her soul surfaced during a session. She had been stuck at two years old, and for years, she didn't even realize it. But as we worked through her healing, something amazing happened. I handed her a soft doll, and she instinctively began stroking it in the manner of a child as she processed—her body remembering something her mind had long buried. The touch unlocked something deep within her, and the healing began.

This is why understanding how memory works is so crucial to inner healing. Trauma doesn't just sit in our minds—it sits in our bodies, in our nervous system, in the very way we see the world. But the beautiful thing is, just as trauma can be stored, healing can be stored, too.

As I grew in my own healing and helped others in theirs, I took a holistic approach, marrying ancient biblical truths with modern understanding of the mind and body. I noted that spiritual realities, human psychology, and the physical makeup of our nervous system can all be reconciled under God's total approach to healing.

This means that *yes*, we believe in instant deliverances, but we also believe in extended times of counsel and processing. Yes, we cleanse the unseen realm that surrounds our lives, but we also take heed to our physical temples, ensuring that we do everything we can to facilitate mental well-being through lifestyle choices.

Some approach healing in a purely materialist way. The problem is, you cannot counsel away a demonic force. Others approach healing purely through a spiritual lens. The problem here is that you cannot cast out a demon that's not there. Not all welfare comes by warfare. This is why the spiritual gift of discernment is so critical for anyone engaging in healing ministry. The cause determines the cure, so if we cannot discern what is causing the pain in someone's life, the cure will elude us. Inner healing is not a one-size-fits-all solution, but a template we can use in cooperation with the Holy Spirit to bring wholeness in any unique case.

At this phase in my life, I did not have a formalized ministry, but these truths were being installed in my approach. Lessons were learned, insight was gained, and God was providing me with outlets and experiences that would become building blocks for my future. While each person I helped had unique situations and traumas, the result of successful healing was always the same: joy unspeakable. I did not have the prophetic insight to see *exactly* where God was taking me, but I did know that joy would follow me wherever I went.

CHAPTER EIGHT
Swapping Coasts

"Go from your country, your people and your father's household to the land I will show you." (Genesis 12:1 NIV)

When God moves you, it's more than a change of scenery. Growth in Him often means leaving behind what's familiar and stepping into places you did not have on your radar. Orange County was my starting soil, but I was a little too comfortable in this garden.

God moves people for different reasons. Sometimes, it's to prepare them for a new assignment, as when He positioned Joseph in Egypt long before he would take on critical roles in government. Other times, it's about spiritual growth—forcing us to leave comfort zones, much like He did with Abraham when He told him to go to an unknown land. He may move us to serve in new territories, just as Esther was placed in Persia *"for such a time as this"* (Esther 4:14). Sometimes, a move is about breaking generational cycles—Lot had to leave Sodom, and Israel had to depart Egypt. And at other times, He moves us for our own protection, as He did when He sent Joseph and Mary to Egypt to protect baby Jesus from Herod's wrath. Beyond all of that, God sometimes moves us—not just for the future but to help us reconcile with the past, to take care of unfinished business, healing, or restoration.

It was on Valentine's Day in 2015, when God spoke to me. I was gearing up for a Saturday night service when the Lord tapped me on the shoulder and said, "Don't go to church tonight. Shut in." By then I was serving closely under Dr. Corral and heavily involved at the church. I obeyed and opened my Bible, landing in Genesis 12—the story of God telling Abraham to leave his country, his family, and everything familiar to go to a land He would show him.

There's a Hebrew concept in that passage: *Lech Lecha*. It means "go to yourself." It's the idea of leaving behind everything that props you up, everything you've leaned on, so that you can discover who you are in God. It's the notion of taking your identity, your insight, your experiences, and carrying them with you to a new land.

As I read those words, the Holy Spirit quickened me. "You're moving," He said.

I was caught off guard but felt a rush of excitement, not dread. I immediately called my cousin, who is also a dear friend, and told her what I was hearing. "I think He's going to move me next year," I said, imagining a gradual, comfortable transition.

It's been said before and bears repeating: God works on His schedule, not ours.

Within a week, I got a call from the higher-ups at ResCare, the company I worked for in Orange County. They told me about a struggling workforce program in Raleigh, North Carolina. The program was losing millions, and they needed someone to go there, assess the situation, and figure out what was going wrong.

I flew to North Carolina a week later. I knew immediately that this wasn't just a temporary assignment. God was moving me to Raleigh and the shift was happening faster than I had anticipated. The program's problems were easy to identify—a management issue that stifled the team's effectiveness—but an answer to prayer came when the head of the Workforce Investment Board walked into my temporary office. For context, the day before, I had asked God to have someone from the board ask me *directly* if God wanted me to move. Confirmation came when the man asked, "Would you consider moving here?"

With the confidence that God was in my corner, I played hardball. "I could—but I would lose a lot with where I'm at. Family, community—the cost of the move. I mean, you guys would have to cover all expenses; it's not cheap to move."

"If we could make it worth your while, would you move here?"

"I would definitely consider it."

When Israel transitioned to Canaan, they left with the riches of Egypt in hand. If God was moving me, I wanted to set my transition up for success. Within a week, the offer was official and the company paid every penny of my moving expenses in a generous relocation package.

It was a brief, bittersweet season of goodbyes. I was saying farewell to my church, my spiritual mom, Dr. Michelle Corral, whose ministry was an incredible lifeline, and a community I loved and had spent a lifetime embedded in. Frankly, before my encounter with Genesis 12, I did not have any intention of leaving California. But here I was, gearing up for a new season in God.

On the day I left, my cousin Michaelyn, who had become a close friend, shot me a text: "God told me you're not moving to Raleigh for Raleigh. He's moving you there to get you closer to the White House."

At the time, a word of that measure was grandiose and tough to believe. I was a bit myopic in my vision but hopeful for what God would do next. Raleigh was a fresh start in every sense of the phrase. The cost of living was better, the pace of life slower, and I felt a new sense of purpose. It's not that I was graduating past my time in California, but I was building upon it. The insights gained at Lyn-Gate Neighborhood Church still remain a sort of spiritual home base for me. The rich, godly conversations I had with my Aunt Nadine and Aunt Allison would continue to replay in my spirit.

North Carolina was a world away from Southern California in many ways—climate, culture, pace, and personality. Where Orange County is sun-soaked and fast-moving, Raleigh has seasons and is unhurried. I adjusted to the sticky summers and small towns. Southern accents replaced diverse SoCal speech. And unlike California, I could find parking anywhere and everywhere.

As an adult living in California, I'd occasionally go to the water—sometimes just to eat at a restaurant with a view of the Pacific. But I didn't fully appreciate the beauty until I moved to North Carolina. Now, when I visit California, I make it a point to go to places such as Newport Coast or Laguna.

As I adjusted to life in the South, it became clear that the reasons for the move were more than a nine-to-five job. I began even more to connect with leaders and grow in what God was calling me into. For several years, I had served various churches and ministries as an intercessor and support. In 2017, I began working with Suzanne Hinn in the area of intercession. She was a prayer warrior, steeped in the traditional approach to spiritual warfare—fasting, long nights of intercession, battling in the spirit. That was the world I knew too.

When I met her husband Benny during a ministry dinner, I expected him to be the same way. But that night, he shared something that changed the way I pray forever. He acknowledged that spiritual warfare had its place, but then he said something profound: "You ladies fight with heavy artillery in the spirit. But I don't fight at all."

That got my attention.

He continued, "When I face battles, I don't go into warfare. I go into the presence of God. I spend time in the glory. And in the glory… there's no fight, the enemy has no access to me."

He went on to share a story about how a U.S. senator once launched a massive investigation against him. It was an unfounded probe, designed to humiliate and to destroy his reputation in the ministry. Summarizing how he handled it, Benny said, "I didn't fight. I didn't defend myself. I just spent time in the presence of Jesus. And in *that* place, God fought for me."

In the end, the investigation resulted in nothing. No wrongdoing. No scandal. No case. The attack collapsed without him lifting a finger. The conversation shook me because it challenged the methodology that I figured was the only way. All my life, I had defaulted to spiritual combat—fighting, rebuking, battling. And yes, there's a time and place for that! But Benny revealed a higher default: living in the presence of God, where the enemy has no foothold.

It changed the way I approach God. Instead of *only* coming with rebukes and requests, I learned to just be with Him. Instead of worrying about attacks, I learned that in His presence, the enemy can't touch me. And when God fights for you, there is no contest. Spiritual warfare is less about the volume and labor involved in my prayers and more about the presence of the One who stands beside me.

The most powerful position a believer can have is a *seated* one. Paul writes that we have been made to *sit* with Christ at the throne. (See Ephesians 2:6.) Yes, we walk, run, fight, and wage war—but our default position is at rest upon the highest throne. This was a major shift in my thinking, because battling and striving had been baked into my DNA from a very young age.

My mother had an unwavering work ethic. To her, everything was about staying on the go. If she saw me sitting on the couch, I was quickly called *lazy*. It wasn't just a passing comment; it became a label—one that nagged at me. Even now, I work very hard—almost never sitting on the couch or taking a rest during the day. From morning until late at night, I'm always occupying myself with something.

There's benefit to such a work ethic, but there's also another side. There's a difference between working hard because you love excellence and working hard to prove you aren't what someone once called you. For a long time, my striving was an attempt to peel off a label. When this is the approach, the label is stubborn and leaves all kinds of residue and mess. When a child is told they are bad, or evil, or lazy, they receive a label that marks them for life unless they seek help. Life's labels seared my heart. As a child, I received every spoken word that was released upon me. My bad behavior was a result of a deeper issue that needed to be addressed. However, if we speak what God says over a child, there is no label to peel off because the label does not exist. A child is not their behavior; the behavior is a result of what's going on inside.

For most of my upbringing, I was never secure in who I was. That insecurity breeds a sense of competition. I wasn't in competition because I wanted to win—I was in competition because I wanted to *matter*. Even spiritually, I felt my mother's competition. She had no problem declaring the anointing of a sibling while downplaying my own to the tune of bluntly saying, "Your sister is anointed. You are not, Sandi."

That kind of environment made me wary of competition later in life. I had to break free from the idea that my worth was tied to productivity. I had to learn that I *do* have a calling, that I *am* anointed. I had to accept that I was not just a word in a dictionary for someone else to define, but that God had established my sense of value long before a curse or hollow word was ever spoken. These lessons and breakthroughs came piece by piece over time. What happened to us is not our fault; however, as adults, it is our responsibility to seek out freedom and healing. We must rise above our past, overcome its weight, and emerge as stronger, better versions of ourselves. God already has this planned for us; we simply need to yield to His process.

The Christian life is more than a prayer for salvation, and it's more than a few sessions of inner healing. Beyond my personal restoration from brokenness, God was plunging the depths of my identity and correcting the ideas I had long believed about myself. He was not just purifying *what* I was doing with my life, but He purified *why* I was doing it. God is not just interested in people serving Him; He is interested in people serving Him for the right reasons. Many ministries have fallen because someone at the helm was doing the work of the Lord without the heart of the Lord. As God progressed me through my new season in the South, I would need both the proper methods and the proper motives in the years to come.

* * *

After some time spent adjusting to North Carolina, God began to bring connections and opportunities. After publishing a prophetic word on Spirit Fuel, I received a call from Brenda, a woman interested in the inner healing process. She was newly relocated from out West, and as we got to know each other, she mentioned that she had attended a church in Colorado that was pastored by a man named Tim Bagwell.

Are you kidding me!?

I had not heard Tim's name in eight years. I explained to her that Tim was the man whose prophecy had shaped and changed my journey. And here I was, being connected to a spiritual daughter of his in my new state. Brenda became a cherished friend and a pillar in my prayer ministry.

It turns out, so much of our spiritual journeys are elliptical. Not *circular*, as if we're endlessly repeating the same thing, but elliptical—where we orbit around certain truths, people, or promises in new and deeper ways each time. That's how God works. He's not recycling things because He ran out of ideas. He's returning to promises because He knows we're finally ready to carry them. In each loop of the ellipse, we're becoming more refined, more rooted, more capable. And as we orbit closer and closer to His heart, we realize—nothing is wasted. Not the waiting, not the wandering, not even the wounds. With each step in my new season, I was reminded afresh of God's careful attention to detail.

Parts of my assignment were new, and others remained the same. For instance, from my childhood—the instinct to fight for the ones who weren't set up for success was built in me. Why? Probably in part because that was me. I know how it feels to start life with the odds stacked against you, to not have the emotional support, ample resources, or a safety net. So whenever I meet someone who's struggling to overcome, my heart leans in. This has remained unwavering in my ministry efforts. But what does it mean for the heart to "lean in"?

I believe it all boils down to one Hebrew word: *chesed*.

In 2 Samuel 9:1, we see a different kind of kindness: *"Now David said, 'Is there still anyone who is left of the house of Saul, that I may show him kindness for Jonathan's sake?'"*

The word *kindness* is the Hebrew word *chesed*. God revealed this passage to me for over two years, and one of the clearest examples of *chesed*—God's lovingkindness—can be seen in King David's relationship with Mephibosheth. David sought out ways to show kindness, and his actions toward Mephibosheth are some of the most profound demonstrations of lovingkindness in the Bible. He wasn't just showing kindness; he was living out *chesed*—a selfless, sacrificial love toward someone who could never repay him.

David was actually known as a *chasid*, a person who regularly embodied *chesed*, going beyond its minimum standard. In Jewish tradition, figures like Honi the Circle Maker, who performed miracles such as praying for rain, are seen as examples of this kind of relationship with God. *Chesed* is about showing kindness to those who cannot return it, and it is at the very heart of God's love. It is also a core theme of Here Comes Joy, as it reflects the deep, unmerited kindness we are called to extend to others.

A perfect example is a young woman I met in another state. She was in her mid-thirties and had survived an abusive mother. She never had a birthday party. Never had anyone celebrate her or fight for her.

Casual kindness might show up as picking up a Hallmark card and scribbling a few well wishes inside. But *chesed*—the kind of lovingkindness that reflects God's heart—calls for more. So a few friends and I gathered a group of women from the local church and threw her a birthday party—her first ever.

They were small gestures, but to her, they meant everything. God used that simple act to bring redemption and healing into her life. She had gone over thirty years without ever being celebrated on her birthday.

Why do I share this? Not because it's some self-congratulatory testimony, but to demonstrate that ministry is not always about grand gestures, six-hour deliverance sessions, or dramatic encounters at the altar. Ministry, at its core, is about presence. It's showing up. It's listening when no one else will and handling practical details that many overlook. There is something sacred about the simple. Beyond world tours and sold-out conferences, there is an artery in the body of Christ carrying willing believers to all kinds of needs. Needs like showing up at the hospital, sending a stack of Valentines and gift cards to single moms without announcing it on social media, buying groceries for the hurting, or praying childlike prayers.

Ordinary is the new extraordinary. You don't need a stage to change someone's life—you need a willing heart. During my time in North Carolina, God was simplifying and clarifying my approach to so many things. I began to see that the simple act of releasing someone to the Lord can equate to years of toil in intercession. I recall praying for a family friend for years. He was a man with a good heart but a penchant for reckless decisions. His charm often overshadowed his missteps as he would make dangerous decisions, and dodge consequences with sheer charisma. My prayers had always centered on his protection, pleading with God to shield him from harm.

However, the Holy Spirit confronted me with a profound question: *Will you entrust him to Me?* That halted me. I cried for an hour as I realized that I felt responsible to save him. I realized that my prayers—though well-intentioned—were attempts to shield him from the very experiences that might lead to real change. I surrendered, knowing that true transformation sometimes requires facing the music.

Days later, he faced a significant setback—losing a six-figure job due to one of these dangerous decisions. Devastated, he reached out to me, which started the beginning of his march toward accountability and growth where his life would make a complete one-eighty. The kind of ministry that changes lives often looks like letting go. It looks like trust.

I observed a common theme in my ministry efforts, whether it was simple intercession, face-to-face inner healing, or declarations for miracles the byproduct was always *joy*. I recall praying for a woman in Raleigh who had been weighed down and pulverized by grief. As I laid my hand on her stomach, she suddenly erupted in laughter—deep, contagious laughter that released a tidal wave throughout the room. Jesus touched her and that joy was more than emotion; it was His restorative force. The heaviness lifted as God moved upon her.

Or even more recently in Brunswick, Georgia. I was with a young lady in a session and in one moment, tears flowed. The next, laughter came so uncontrollably that I couldn't help but join in. The room erupted, joy spread like wildfire, and my spirit shouted the only fitting response:

"When your money is funny and your change is strange, God's gonna give you...*joy!*"

On another occasion, we had a weekend inner healing retreat at a lake just north of Charlotte, North Carolina. A group of about fifteen ladies were gathered. When it came time for ministry, we began to worship and get into the presence of God. The Lord moved so sweetly upon women in a life-changing way. One lady with the most beautiful red hair stood out to me. She was sitting on the floor further away from the group, enjoying time with the Lord. I knew God wanted to touch her in a special way, specifically by going back in time to heal her childhood. She happened to work in a helping profession and had a successful practice. In truth, the ones who spend their days pouring into others often need a touch from God the most.

I came over, sat by her, and the Holy Spirit said, *Hold her.*

God began to touch her as I held her while we both sat on the floor. I shared with her what God was showing me about her childhood. Something happened and she began to cry, and that crying turned to weeping, and weeping turned to sobbing. She was encountering Jesus and grieving something that I had no idea about. I knew the Holy Spirit was touching her and she was receiving freedom that she had waited a long time for. I'm not sure how long we stayed there in that embrace, but judging by the fact that my leg went numb, my arm fell asleep, and my neck was stuck in a questionable position—I'd say it was a while.

After the grieving was finished, she went quiet. A few minutes of silence followed, and God showed me that she had been a spiritual midwife to so many and had broken others free. Now, He brought a midwife to break her free. She turned to me with a very serious look and said, "What took you so long?" We both broke out in boisterous laughter that lingered, and lingered for at least twenty minutes. The Holy Spirit induced a laughter that lit up the home and others broke out in laughter as well on the other side of the room while worshiping. It was a Jesus-Joy fest. Freedom was in the house and His name was and is *Jesus*.

Testimony after testimony resulted in joy unspeakable, joy undeniable, joy unstoppable. Joy was the exclamation mark on the end of a heavy sentence that preceded it. The word, and the essence of it, became a banner over my ministry. It clarified my calling and formed my future.

PART 3

Propelled into Promise

CHAPTER NINE

Platforms

"Joy is the serious business of heaven." —*C.S. Lewis*

It's 2018, and I am hearing persistent whispers from God to start my own ministry. I resist at every turn. Anyone watching my life in those years would bear witness to the fact that I was actively involved in doing the work of ministry left and right—I just had not formalized an organization of my own. At this point, I was no longer working in workforce services. Instead, I had transitioned to part-time work with Susanne Hinn and was also contributing remotely to the Elijah List. However, I began to feel a sense of separation from both roles, something I couldn't quite explain. It was as if I could no longer rekindle the same sense of belonging I once had. It felt like God was preparing my heart for my ministry, even before the events that would bring it to fruition. This is often how God works in my life—He introduces a sense that something greater is on the horizon, even before I can fully comprehend what lies ahead.

As I helped with special projects for various ministries around the country, with each new season, the whisper remained, "Start your own ministry."

Who would want to hear what I have to say? I thought.

God kept pressing, and I began to toy with the idea in my mind. I knew *breakthrough* was and would be a key part of my calling. We hear a lot about breakthroughs in church circles, but I've come to learn it's more than a buzzword. It is more than a feeling or a high point in worship. It's that threshold where something finally shifts irreversibly. The weight lifts. The wall comes down. It's when what's been stuck or blocked suddenly gives, and God moves in a way you can't deny. It's God splitting the sea. It's Goliath hitting the dirt.

As these themes and realities swirled in my spirit, I got a phone call out of the blue from Steve Schultz, President of the Elijah List. He said, "I spoke to God about you, and He told me it's time for you to start your own ministry."

It confirmed the months of wrestling I had done in private. God delivered the word to me so that I would not be afraid to step out and take the leap. Having Steve's blessing meant a lot, and I left Elijah List to officially launch the ministry. I asked the Lord, "What do I name this?" Psalm 45:7 came to mind: *"You have loved righteousness and hated iniquity; therefore, God, your God, has anointed you with the oil of joy above your companions."*

I heard the Lord say, "Here Comes Joy."

At first, I hesitated. I thought people might assume I was indicating that the name was about *me*, when it is about the arrival of Jesus in our lives. It was about the joy that comes when the enemy's hold is broken.

Launching Here Comes Joy was the furthest thing from an overnight event. For decades, I had been through seasons of crushing, healing, despair, restoration, agony, fire, wholeness, and everything in between. Nothing was wasted. The darkness taught me how to embrace His light, and the low points taught me how to lean heavily on God.

In starting the ministry, I could see that I now carried an authority in so many areas—to break people free from the bondage that I had known in my own story. God is so beautiful in that way. That which the enemy uses to try to destroy us is often transformed by God into tools of delivery for others. I believe many organizations, businesses, and even families can fail because of a tendency toward the "ready, fire, aim" approach. People leap before they have learned, and they try to heal before being made whole. If church history has taught us anything, it's that gifting can take you somewhere, but your character will keep you there. Talent can open doors, but it's character that keeps them open.

Biblically, God anoints those with character. David was chosen by God and anointed, not just because he was the young guy in the field who people overlooked, but because he had a heart after the Lord. Anointing comes to us, not just because there is a job to do, but because there is a holy heart that can steward that anointing. Years of crushing had prepared me for my calling. It's more than behavior modification—it's a gradual reset of beliefs, perspectives, and perceptions. For instance, discovering my prophetic gift did not happen in the blink of an eye. Growing up in a home where someone thought they heard from God—but often wasn't hearing from Him—had left me with a distaste for anything remotely "prophetic." I didn't trust it, and I certainly didn't want to misuse it.

However, encountering mentors like Dr. Corral, who operated in the prophetic with humility and accuracy, began to break my disillusionment. She helped restore my trust in God's gifts and their place in the body. Joining her prayer team and working alongside seasoned intercessors had really nurtured my growth. I began to see in the spirit and hear words and phrases that I could verbalize in the organic flow of prayer and prophecy. All of these things I carried with me as *Here Comes Joy* got off the ground.

I learned from the good and the bad alike. God's poetic justice is always at work. He uses the very things that could have destroyed us to refine us. Even after I began in ministry, I saw leaders within the body of Christ who exhibited qualities different from Christ. Over the years, God positioned me to see leaders who were steeped in pride so that I could see its destructive nature and reject it in my own life. Echoing David when he saw the wickedness in Saul, God used my early experiences in ministry to crush the things in me that didn't align with Him. It wasn't just about producing oil in the crushing of the olive press—it was about removing anything in me that could become a stumbling block later. He was preparing me for something greater, and that preparation required development. And, there were plenty of unhealed places for the Lord to refine in me.

But that's not always easy.

That refining often shows up in unexpected places—sometimes even in the middle of ministry opportunities that appear to be open doors. Years ago, while visiting Southern California, a friend invited me to participate in a prophetic presbytery during a conference that a well-known ministry was hosting. I had never been directly involved with this ministry, but I was excited—it focused on the prophetic gifts of God, which had always been a passion of mine. I'd heard wonderful things about them, even though I hadn't followed the particular minister closely.

When I arrived, we were paired up in twos as the conference broke for lunch, and attendees lined up to receive prophetic ministry. I grabbed my anointing oil—something that had become a regular companion during live ministry—and began praying for each person alongside my ministry partner. About twenty minutes in, a kind lady who worked for the ministry gently pulled me aside.

"Hello there," she said softly. "I've noticed that everyone you pray for starts to cry."

I smiled and replied, "Well, yes, that happens when God begins healing them. I'm not just a 'word' person—God often sets people free in more ways than one."

Right then, I started to feel a little self-conscious. It was becoming clear I didn't quite fit the flow of their ministry style. *Was I out of place?*

She continued, still very kind, "You're doing great, but we try not to make people cry—we focus more on giving them an encouraging word."

I was a little confused but nodded as she went on. "Also, the anointing oil... it feels a bit old-fashioned for this setting. We have a lot of people here from Los Angeles—many in the creative arts and Hollywood—and we try not to overwhelm anyone."

A wave of emotion hit me. I didn't know how to respond. But instinctively, I leaned into what I had been taught—the Word, and the ways of *chesed*, God's covenant love and kindness. I simply smiled, nodded, and thanked her for the feedback.

Even though I felt embarrassed and unsure how to offer the kind of "happy, joyful" encouragement they preferred, I couldn't ignore what I knew deep down: that true freedom often involves more than just encouragement. It involves an encounter. It involves the Holy Spirit. From that experience, I learned something crucial: I have a very specific calling. And that kind of calling often brings resistance. The enemy doesn't mind if you go to church, read your

Bible, or follow the rules. But when people start breaking free, the resistance gets real.

A second realization followed, and it was just as important: faithfulness to the ministry and the anointing God gives you is non-negotiable. We are not called to convenience or popularity—we're called to obedience. I'm not here to win a crown; I'm here to host the King. I'm not called to be liked or to tone things down when Jesus shows up.

Yes, we should always avoid strife, especially when we're guests under someone else's leadership. But we also need to recognize that we won't always fit in the boxes of others. Loyalty to God and His commission must guide where we serve, how we minister, and who we partner with. If we keep reshaping ourselves to meet everyone's expectations, we'll eventually dilute the gospel and lose the approval of the One who matters most.

We need to be okay with being unfriended—even by influential people who choose polish and composure over the presence and power of God.

At the end of the day, I had to ask myself: *Who am I more afraid of disappointing—people, or God?*

The answer was clear.

I'd rather stand alone in truth than be surrounded by people who require my silence.

Experiences of this nature remind me why I'm so careful with trust. It's not about paranoia; it's about wisdom. Trust is a gift, and once it's violated, it can be a challenge to repair. I was quickly learning that ministry is not just about those you are ministering *to*, but those you are ministering *with*.

Who are you standing beside? What team are you locking arms with?

Over time, God has clarified and unified those with whom Here Comes Joy partners.

A fruitful connection I've had has been with Lance Wallnau and his ministry. That connection began at the 2017 Inaugural Gala, where I had been helping organize the event. The organization I worked for at the time was mulling back and forth about who should be on stage, and I strongly recommended Lance. At the time, Lance had a huge following on Periscope, where he was breaking down current events, discussing politics, and helping shape the Christian response to what was happening in America. I voiced, "You have to have this guy speak. He's influencing thousands of people daily, and he's going to help turn the tide."

They were hesitant at first, but after watching some of his Periscope broadcasts, they were sold. Lance was invited to speak at the gala, and from there, I developed a friendship with his wife, Annabelle. Over the years, our paths continued to cross. I'd be involved in various ministry projects, and Lance or Annabelle would be a part of them. One year, I was working with a foundation that wanted to bless Lance's ministry with a grant, and I was able to make the connection for them.

Slowly, trust was built.

A few years later, I had a dream that I was working for Lance and Annabelle. In the dream, it was the election year, and there was a lot of turmoil and harassment coming against Lance's ministry. In the dream, I was behind the scenes, helping and supporting them. Just two months later, I got a call from Lance's business partner, Mercedes, saying they wanted to bring me on board to help with the Courage Tour and partner development. The dream had come to pass *exactly* as God had shown me. Even though I was fully immersed and busy in ministry within *Here Comes Joy*, I felt that this was a special assignment that I had to take on as well. Obedience is greater than sacrifice.

Lance's ministry was growing exponentially, and I came on board at exactly the right time. I helped with special projects, intercession, and partner development, ensuring that the work God is doing through the ministry was supported in every dimension. So in a sense, Here Comes Joy was not just a ministry in and of itself but a ministry to ministries.

In 2018, I had been introduced to Centered for Life Counseling Center in Georgia, and through prayer calls and consultations, I began to form a relationship. By 2019, that evolved into a full working partnership. Beyond that, I had contracted with Vision Television, Georgian Banov, Elijah Streams Television, Evangelist Alveda King, and others. From Fox and Friends, CTN, The Elijah List, The Newscasters Network to Spirit Fuel and other publications. God was providing global platforms.

Years before, a prophet told me, "Your forefathers rubbed shoulders with kings, and so will you." I thought back to my grandfather, William McGuire, who was a chief and a man of influence in his time. But this was not about chasing people of influence. It was about chasing the heart of God. As I pursued Him, He naturally placed me in rooms I hadn't thought to enter. He aligned me with the very people I was destined to serve alongside.

I remember a minister once telling me, "Sandi, if you were dropped in Zambia with nothing, you would still attract people of influence. If you were placed among the Aborigines in Australia, you would be connected with leaders in no time." The reality is, while big platforms are a privilege, they should always be taken with caution, and never apart from where the Holy Spirit is leading.

* * *

When the influence of a ministry grows, there can be a temptation for the founder's ego to grow with it. Rubbing shoulders with people in high places can cause us to lose sight of humility if we aren't careful. The same thing is true with a gift from the Lord. If we replace God with the gift He gave, our downfall is on the way.

Influence, opportunity, positions, and gifts all have their place, but they are *supplemental* in nature. When they become the *substance* of our identity, we lose sight of the God who gave them. I began to notice something happening as a regular part of my ministry output: as I prayed, God moved. At first, I admit, I got caught up in the excitement of discovering my gifts. I wanted to use them and to walk in the anointing. But God had to slow me down a bit to teach me a crucial lesson: *your identity is not in your gifts. It's not about what you can offer or do—it's about who I say you are.*

There's a temptation to attach your identity to your abilities, your relationships, or your achievements. At times, I found myself with one foot in that trap, especially when I began running in influential circles. Early on, I was so excited to be connected to high-profile leaders. I'd post photos on social media, thinking, "Look at me, I've arrived!" But God, in His grace, began to dismantle that pride in me. More than once, for special projects, God placed me under a prideful leader, which remedied my pride quickly.

God has a way of breaking down the things we build our identity on. He had to strip away my reliance on external validation. Whether it was the people I was around or the gifts I carried, none of those things could define my worth. My value comes solely from who God says I am and what Christ did for me. If the cross of Jesus is not a sufficient validation of our worth, we are not in a position to proclaim that cross. How can we preach a gospel that we ourselves are not fully satisfied with?

At first, I didn't realize I was placing my sense of worth in the wrong things. But God used those moments to teach me. I realized that the pictures, the connections, the name-dropping—they were symptoms of a deeper insecurity. He had to excavate everything I'd built my foundation on and rebuild it on Him alone.

God was relentlessly working in me and through me. Eventually, I ran myself ragged trying to prove I was called. I was saying yes to everything, showing up for everyone, pouring out constantly without pausing to check in with my own soul. I thought hustle meant obedience, and obedience meant hustle. Somewhere in my soul, I held the lie that exhaustion was just part of the assignment. But over time, I realized I was mistaking drive for anointing. I was overworking, not because God demanded it, but because I was still trying to earn what had already been freely given.

Before COVID happened, the Lord said He was going to slow me down. At the time, I didn't realize I had put all of my value in being busy, needed, and sought after. For decades, I prided myself on being independent. As a coping mechanism to my childhood pain, I learned to become *needless and wantless*. I suppressed my own fundamental needs and desires to avoid being disappointed, as I experienced so often in the past. I built a fortress around myself—not in an aggressive way, but in a quiet, intentional, "I've got this" kind of way. I didn't ask for help. I didn't let people see when I was struggling, and I thought strength meant independence.

A moment of transformation came in 2020 when I had to go in for surgery. At the time, the hospital had strict rules—you *had* to have someone drop you off, stay in the hospital through the surgery, pick you up, and monitor you at home for the first 24 hours. There was no Ubering home and no handling it solo. Not wanting to inconvenience anyone, the only option I was comfortable with was my cousin, who was also independent, fully grasping the strong-woman's creed. She was supposed to fly in, but at the last minute, her husband suffered a medical emergency. Every other backup plan crumbled. It almost seemed divinely orchestrated that I would now have to reach outside of my comfort zone, face to face with a level of vulnerability that I wasn't used to.

I reached out to Ben, a friend who ran a local prayer room in Raleigh, and asked if he had any trusted friends in ministry who could help with this need. This was no small ask, as it would require someone very safe in order for me to allow them in my personal space. Ben had the perfect person, Natalie. She was beyond what I had asked for, a woman who lives in the presence of God, and it shows throughout her life.

She drove me to the hospital and remained close, ensuring that I felt comfortable. It meant a great deal to have her there. There we were in the preparation room before heading into surgery. This situation made me feel incredibly vulnerable. Fear of the unknown shows up in funny ways. Here I was with not one person who actually knew me. Everything that could identify me was taken away, from my driver's license to my clothing to my phone. I was lying on a gurney no different than the day I was born. Heading into the operating room, it was just me, Jesus, and Natalie. Instances like this test a person's identity.

I was more thankful than I could express to have Natalie by my side. It was the first time in a long time that I had let someone see me in a completely helpless state. And you know what? The world didn't end. No one kicked me while I was down or abandoned me. If anything, it developed a great friendship between Natalie and me. To this day, she and her husband Tyrone are close friends. God delivered me through the surgery with abundant grace. Over the next few days, more friends dropped by, and I quickly regained strength. God was faithful, and He used this predicament to shed light on my commitment to being needless and wantless to cope when I felt unprotected. Vulnerability did not destroy me. And it won't destroy you either.

I think back to those two weeks often. Because if God has been teaching me anything over these years, it's that strength isn't about never needing people. It's about knowing *who* you can need. As much as I've fought for others, I'm learning that sometimes, I need to let them fight for me too.

Since then, I've made a conscious effort to embrace vulnerability. I've seen the difference it makes, even in ministry. With Here Comes Joy, I've found that the more open and real I am with my team, the stronger the community becomes. When I allow myself to be human—to admit when I need help, to invite others into the process—it creates space for deeper trust.

There was a time when I believed that keeping people at arm's length would protect me. But now I see that living behind walls is its own kind of prison. And ironically, that's exactly what I had told myself I *never* wanted to be—closed off, fearful of new opportunities, unwilling to embrace change.

As we exited the COVID era, change was coming. For years, my ministry had taken me across the country—California, Texas, Arizona, Oregon, Georgia, Virginia, the Dakotas. But one day, the Lord spoke to me clearly: "You are going to plow in your own backyard. The way is open."

At that point, I had done very little ministry in Raleigh—my actual home base. I was comfortable traveling to minister elsewhere or speaking at someone else's meeting. Hosting my own event was a different level of vulnerability. *What if no one shows up?* I wondered.

Despite my fears, I obeyed. At the beginning of the year, I rented a small community center and released a social media invitation. I didn't know what to expect, but God showed up. The woman who ran the center was a Christian who had been praying for a ministry to come for some time. People drove in from neighboring cities. And within three days, I received a phone call from a church in Durham, offering their building for monthly meetings—completely free of charge. I had no marketing plan, no network, and no established reputation in the area. But because I obeyed, God made the way.

Since then, these meetings have been incredibly fruitful. We've seen breakthrough, deliverance, and the fire of God fall time and time again. I've been able to observe and take note of what God is doing through Here Comes Joy. I can't help but see myself as a spiritual midwife, of sorts. Discernment, whether in a big meeting or a private one, is a critical tool for diagnostics. Then, at times, I feel the Spirit of God releasing a hammer, breaking through barriers. At other times, He's more gentle and precise, healing trauma and oppression.

Not every ministry is meant to look the same. Paul reminded us in 1 Corinthians that the body has many parts—each one with a unique role to play. The hand doesn't try to be the eye, and the ear doesn't envy the foot. In the same way, every ministry carries a distinct, heaven-ordained assignment. Some are called to preach the Gospel in stadiums. Others to disciple in small living rooms. And some, like Here Comes Joy, are designed to walk people into breakthrough and wholeness.

Here Comes Joy isn't just about teaching or deliverance from a platform. It's not just intercession, inner healing, or ministry meetings. It's *all* of those things, woven together. The approach is deeply holistic. We deal with spiritual strongholds, yes—but we also address impact on the body and the nervous system. We lead people in prayer, and we also give them tools to process their emotions, identify lies they've believed, and renew their minds. We war and we rest. We speak truth boldly, and we whisper prayers over quiet hearts. It's not all fire and fervor—and it's not all softness and serenity either. Yes, it's a corporate gathering, and it's face-to-face engagement. Why? One, because real freedom isn't found in just one area—it's found when all the pieces come together and align with God's truth. And two, because this was my story also. My journey of healing has been more than a single prayer for deliverance and has transcended a solely practical approach to mental health.

In fact, in the next chapter, I'll walk you through some of the most powerful areas of ministry that not only shaped my own healing but have now become tools I use to help others find freedom. These aren't just methods or formulas—they're revelations that were refined in the fire of my own story. What God taught me in the valley, I now carry into every session, every encounter at the altar, and every fervent prayer with someone who feels lost or broken.

It's one of the greatest privileges of my life—to take what once nearly destroyed me and offer it back to others as healing oil. So if you're reading this, wondering if your pain can serve a greater purpose—keep reading. The very places the enemy tried to bury you might be the ground where your ministry is planted.

CHAPTER TEN
Innerworkings

"I am not what happened to me, I am what I choose to become." – C.G. Jung

Touching a coffin. Putting fingers in ears. A mixture of spit and mud on the eyes. A word from a distance. Uttering a simple phrase. All of these (and more) were methods used in the ministry of Jesus to bring about physical healing. Each of these shows that healing with Jesus was relational, not ritual. He tailored His approach to the person's need—and regularly used the *unusual* to spark wonder and build faith. When we fast forward through the New Testament, we see even more variation: anointing oil, handkerchiefs, or the shadow of Peter.

If God's approach to physical healing and deliverance is so varied, how much more multifaceted is the approach to emotional well-being? In my life, trauma came in all sorts of shapes and sizes, from emotional and physical abuse to a string of deaths. As a result, my healing came in all sorts of shapes and sizes. As people being healed and as people in a position to help heal others, we cannot lean on just one modality. When we do, it's similar to dressing a wound with a single bandage and refusing to revisit, disinfect, or redress. The pursuit of wholeness isn't one-size-fits-all.

To this point, you've read my accounts of trauma and the healing that came subsequently, but it's worth taking some time to look at the inner workings of healing. Here you'll see both my own steps toward wholeness and the various approaches we might use or recommend within Here Comes Joy. Therapy is an incredibly valuable resource for all. Of course, it can be misused or misappropriated like any other good thing in life. If individuals expect it to cure every problem by replacing repentance, obedience, or biblical living, then we are off to a bad start. However, these methods of healing, paired with accountability and a Spirit-led lifestyle, can radically revolutionize your world.

Inner Healing

One of the most life-changing inner healing models I've encountered—and now use in my ministry—is called *Restoring the Foundations* (RTF). When I first stepped into this process, I was desperate for wholeness, but also cautious. I didn't want just another spiritual bandage or a hype-filled experience that wore off the next day. I needed something deep, lasting, and rooted in truth. If an inner healing ministry is aligned with heaven, that's exactly what you will experience in the process.

Restoring the Foundations is based on a biblical worldview that addresses four key areas that tend to hold people back from freedom: ungodly beliefs, generational patterns, life's wounding experiences, and demonic oppression. It's holistic—meaning it doesn't treat symptoms in isolation, but looks at the whole person. I appreciated that. As someone who grew up in a dysfunctional environment, I had layers of unresolved pain. RTF didn't rush me. It walked me step-by-step through identifying the root systems behind the fruit in my life.

A biblical worldview is absolutely central to this process. Without it, inner healing can drift into basic self-help or even New Age thinking. What I loved about RTF is that it kept Jesus at the center. It's not about fixing yourself—it's about allowing the Holy Spirit to reveal truth, apply healing, and bring transformation. I learned that many of my core beliefs were simply wrong—things I'd internalized growing up in survival mode. You may have grown up in church and feel as if you have all of your doctrinal ducks in a row—but even then, you'd be surprised at the little beliefs you've allowed to take hold in your thinking. If you believe a lie, you empower the liar. RTF gave me a grid for identifying those false beliefs, forgiving where needed, renouncing lies, and replacing them with God's truth.

One particular area of RTF that helped me was breaking ungodly soul ties. Ungodly Soul ties occur when a person has too much influence or the wrong kind of influence in our lives. This influence may come from co-dependency, control, manipulation, or intimidation in an attempt to take away your free will. Ungodly soul ties can be created in a number of ways, including a sexual partner other than a spouse. After breaking soul ties from those who hurt me, I gained freedom from the memories of pain and shame. This shut off the access that the enemy used to allow people to have a hold on me. Breaking ungodly soul ties involves a very simple prayer that releases a great deal of heaviness we carry emotionally and spiritually.

In addition to the release from ungodly soul ties, the benefits of RTF for me were many. Freedom. Clarity. A greater sense of identity. I felt lighter—mentally, emotionally, and spiritually. I wasn't walking around with invisible weights anymore. I also noticed a greater authority in prayer and ministry, because when you've been through deliverance and inner healing yourself, you carry that breakthrough for others.

Without a model like RTF—or some biblical framework for healing—I think a lot of people stay stuck. They go to church, they love God, but they don't understand why they can't break free from certain patterns. They wonder why relationships keep failing or why anxiety keeps knocking at their door. You can be saved and still struggle. Inner healing isn't about your salvation—it's about your restoration and appropriating what Christ did for you on the Cross. And for me, inner healing was one of the most powerful tools on that journey. It wasn't flashy. It wasn't fast. But it was a foundation that I still build on today—and it's a foundation we actively help pour for others in our ministry. Wholeness is a lifelong journey of discovering and securing your true identity in Christ.

EMDR Therapy

A major part of my trauma was carrying painful memories I had no idea how to process. A memory is more than a mental picture of the past. It's a force of influence on the present. Even if you stuff them away and pretend they don't exist, they are indirectly guiding behaviors. For me, Eye Movement Desensitization and Reprocessing (EMDR) provided a path of reconciling with traumatic memories and healing my dissociation. EMDR is a psychotherapy approach that alleviates the distress associated with traumatic memories. It's been around since the late 1980s and has seen some incredible results. Studies have shown that up to 90% of individuals with single-event trauma no longer have PTSD symptoms after just three 90-minute EMDR sessions. Another study reported that 77% of combat veterans were free of PTSD after 12 sessions[2].

How does it work? First of all, it's important to note that there's nothing spooky or mystical about it. EMDR facilitates the processing of traumatic experiences through guided eye movements or taps. This bilateral stimulation allowed me to revisit painful moments from my past but to

---

2. The Trauma Practice. "What Is EMDR Therapy & Does It Work?" Last modified approximately 6.3 years ago. Accessed April 1, 2025. https://traumapractice.co.uk/does-emdr-work

integrate these memories in a healthy way. It helped me reconnect with parts of myself that had gone numb. It didn't erase the memories, but it took the sting out of them. I was able to look at the past *objectively* and not just as a series of events that I was a victim of. It was like God took those painful moments, gently rearranged how my brain was holding them, and said, "See? I was with you there, too."

Today, I often recommend EMDR to others walking through their healing. In the end, it enables individuals to integrate these memories more adaptively. EMDR does not replace faith; it deepens it. If God could use a donkey to deliver truth (see Numbers 22), I think He can use a practitioner and a neuroscience-backed method to bring His children into wholeness.

I was first introduced to it by Debby Temmer, CEO of Centered for Life counseling center in Saint Simons Island, Georgia. During one particular EMDR session, we were exploring my patterns in relationships. I tended to enter into relationships, only to sabotage them. I would go on a few dates, and then, without fail, I would find a reason to walk away. My friend Shea once pointed it out to me: "You start building a case against people you date *immediately*." At first, I laughed it off, but during EMDR, we dug deeper.

As I followed the therapy's process, a memory surfaced—the day my father left. The pain hit me with the force of a wave. At that moment, I realized that somewhere deep inside, I had formed a core belief: *"All men will always leave me."* It wasn't something I had consciously decided. It was something my heart had learned through experience. And because I believed it, I expected it—a self-fulfilling prophecy began a nasty loop. I spent my life waiting for men to leave, so much so that I made sure to leave them first. My case against the men I knew was a defensive mechanism, not some conscious effort to stay alone.

It was a heartbreaking realization, but it made so much sense. My father's abandonment had created a filter through which I saw every man who entered my life. Subconsciously, I was reliving that same wound over and over again. EMDR not only helped me to identify that root issue, but also to modify my approach in the days and years to come.

Somatic Experiencing

Dr. Barbara Lowe was a facilitator of Somatic Experiencing, which had a significant impact on my healing. Ultimately, it helped me release trauma that was deeply stored in my body—tensions, fears, and anxieties I'd carried for years. Trauma isn't just something held in our memories; it can also reside in our muscles, our posture, and our very breathing.

Through guided exercises, I learned to listen carefully to what my body was telling me. Dr. Lowe taught me to recognize physical sensations tied to emotional memories, to approach them with kindness and curiosity, and to allow those sensations to release. With each session, layers of accumulated tension melted away, replaced by a sense of safety and ease. I found myself breathing more deeply, standing taller, and living with a newfound physical and emotional freedom.

It was in these sessions that I came face-to-face with the sexual assault I had experienced in high school. The weight of that night had impacted my soul and body for decades in a heavy silence. Following this assault, I had dissociated[3] from my own body and lived many years without awareness of why I couldn't look at myself in the mirror without cringing. Within the sessions, I had room to process and heal—eliminating the shame toward my body that I had maintained until then. Psalm 46:10 says, *"Be still, and know that I am God."* Somatic Experiencing helped me embrace

---

3. Dissociation is a mental process where a person feels disconnected from their thoughts, feelings, memories, or sense of identity.

stillness, not as passive waiting, but as an active posture of trust and surrender.

What all of these modalities of healing brought is *awareness*. Awareness is everything. Many people who struggle to build healthy relationships or find healing from their past have one major issue: a lack of self-awareness. You cannot resolve what you do not recognize. Half the battle is simply identifying the cause. If water is flooding your house, identifying where it's coming from is an urgent matter. Shutting off the valve is not overly complicated, once you know where the water is coming from.

These various sessions with different methods all brought me to a heightened sense of awareness. They also all had a common theme: they were conducted in the presence of a safe person. A counselor, therapist, or inner healing minister creates an environment where wounds can be revisited, but this time, in safety. When someone carries deep trauma, they often lack a safe adult at the time of the wounding. This is why it's so critical to allow reconciliation work to take place with a safe, trusted expert. Many times, a person carries shame from their trauma, believing on some level that they deserved what happened to them. A good therapist or inner healing minister can speak the truth: "You didn't deserve that. You needed love.

You needed protection." And often, that simple validation leads to a flood of emotion and deep healing.

When we look at Jesus, we see the same pattern. He didn't just correct people—He comforted them. He validated their pain, spoke the truth, and restored their dignity. Inner healing is simply a continuation of the work He began. When I first started doing this work, I made the mistake of overstepping at times. I thought I needed to fix everyone who crossed my path. If I saw a wound, I jumped in, ready to apply the balm. But over time, I've learned that not everyone is ready for healing—and my attempts to "help" could actually do more harm than good.

That's why, within Here Comes Joy, I have a strict policy now: I only work with people who seek me out. If someone calls and says, "Can I send so-and-so to you for a session?" My answer is always the same: "They have to call me themselves." Healing can't be forced. If someone isn't willing to take the first step, they're likely not ready.

There's also a matter of impact. As someone in a leadership role, I'm acutely aware of how my words and actions can affect others. If I approach someone who isn't ready and suggest they need healing, I risk bringing shame into the equation—and shame is never a path to freedom. It's a delicate dance, knowing when to step in and when to step back, and I lean on the Holy Spirit to guide me. Inner healing is always a dance between experience, observation, and the Holy Spirit's gentle nudges. There are windows when my training helps me recognize patterns and connect dots, but the real breakthroughs come when I step back and let Him lead.

I've seen God move in ways that defy logic. There have been moments when I thought, *This person isn't ready. This breakthrough feels impossible.* But I've prayed anyway, trusting God to do what only He can do. And time and time again, He surprises me.

I've witnessed Him reach into the deepest corners of a person's heart—places even they didn't know existed—and bring healing that leaves us both in awe. I'm convinced that God desires our freedom even more than we do. He's already paid the price.

My role is simply to help create a space where people feel safe, loved, and seen—because when they do, their hearts begin to open, and God meets them there.

* * *

"Lord, I have nothing. If You don't show up, we're all sunk."

This is the simple admission that I pray at the start of any inner healing session. It's not false humility; it's the absolute truth. No matter how much training or experience I've had, I know real breakthrough only happens when the Holy Spirit moves.

Inner healing is as much about listening as it is about guiding. It's not my job to tell someone what's wrong or how to fix it. People don't find freedom because they're handed the answers. They find freedom when they come to their own revelations, when the truth hits their spirit and resonates deep in their hearts.

It's comparable to being an attorney in a courtroom. You don't tell the witness what to say; you ask the right questions, leading them to the realization they need. For example, someone might come into a session and tell me, "Oh, I had a great childhood. My relationship with my mom is perfect—we're best friends!"

At face value, that sounds wonderful. But if I sense there's more under the surface, I'll gently probe. "That's great," I'll say. "Can you tell me how your mom shows you love?" That's often when the cracks begin to show. Their response might reveal a pattern of behavior or an unmet need they hadn't consciously recognized. And once they see it, they're ready to break free. Because in reality, I've come to realize that what people *say* is only part of the story. Words are powerful, yes, but they're often a mask, a way of protecting ourselves or presenting a version of reality that feels safer to share. What I'm really listening for is the heart—the beliefs and experiences that live beneath the surface, influencing how we see the world and ourselves.

The true thoughts and feelings of the heart usually live behind a veil. I often say that healing requires stepping through the "thin veil" of vulnerability. It's that moment where everything in you wants to hold back, to stay safe and hidden, but if you can just take the risky step, there's freedom on the other side. The ones who struggle the most, who can't seem to find healing, are often the ones who aren't ready to be vulnerable. It's not that they don't want to heal—they do—but they're afraid of what they'll find if they let go of their defenses. But when someone is willing to take that step, when they allow themselves to be seen and known, that's when real healing begins. It's in that place of surrender that God meets us.

One of the most fascinating aspects of this work is how the Holy Spirit reveals things to me—sometimes in ways I can't explain. It's the synergy between therapeutic practices and prophetic insight. I remember one time texting my assistant after a trip, "Did you get home safe?" and she replied with a simple *yes*.

But as soon as I read her text, I felt a sharp pain in my stomach. I couldn't ignore it. "Hey," I texted back, "is your stomach okay?"

She responded, "How did you know? I don't remember telling you."

She hadn't told me. The Holy Spirit did. This sort of thing happens to me all the time. If someone has an ailment, I'll often feel it in my own body—an ache, a twinge, a pressure—and I know it's an invitation to pray. Once, I was sitting in a Starbucks texting a friend. She mentioned she was at the doctor, and suddenly I felt a stabbing pain in my lower back, so intense I could hardly stand. I began to pray, and the pain subsided after about an hour. Later, she told me she was being treated for a kidney issue—exactly where I'd felt the pain.

Discernment is critical. In this kind of ministry, you have to bring an entire toolbox to the table. Sometimes a word of knowledge from the Lord is needed; other times it requires an unorthodox integration led by the Holy Spirit. As mentioned before, I've sat with people who were mentally stuck in childhood. They had adult lives and duties, but were stunted and stuck in a juvenile state. At times, I will hand the person a slinky and encourage them to play with it. The bilateral motion stimulates two sides of the brain, and suddenly, we are integrating memories and seasons of early life that can be felt, dealt with, and made whole.

When I first began inner healing work, I leaned heavily on resources like *Restoring the Foundations* and the Townsend and Cloud model, which focuses on addressing the root issues rather than the symptoms. I attended the One Week Intensive (OWI) at the Townsend Institute, which was a transformative experience for me. It was held at the Ayres Hotel & Suites in Costa Mesa, California, and this five-day program accelerated personal and professional growth for me and other counselors in their roles. Throughout the week, I participated in teaching sessions led by experts, including Townsend and Cloud themselves. Their insights into the Growth Model and the integration of biblical principles with current neuroscience deeply clicked with me.

A significant component of the OWI was the nine process groups run by highly trained professionals. These sessions allowed me to delve into my own character development, confront obstacles, and apply the teachings in a supportive environment. Their concept of "root change equals fruit change" has stayed with me. By the end of the week, I had not only gained valuable tools and techniques to enhance my ministry's effectiveness but also undergone a wonderful personal transformation.

Over the years, God has expanded my "toolbox" through hands-on experiences, programs, and His faithful leading. There are a number of qualities required for anyone who is positioned to help others, and one of them is the quality of being a lifelong learner. Even as a child, I saw God in the miracle of science. I marveled at the intricacies of creation, from the stars in the sky to the wonders of the ocean. Even today, I continue to marvel over the detailed makeup of human life and God's plan to heal: spirit, soul, and body. If the Biblical narrative has taught us anything, it's that we once were lost, and now we are found. It's the inner healing process in its various forms that moves us from merely being found to *flourishing*.

It's important to clarify that while methods matter, they must never replace the move of the Holy Spirit. Lately, I've seen the Holy Spirit move powerfully, even without using any specific modalities or techniques. One example comes to mind: a friend and client of mine, a singer-songwriter, asked for a session before recording her first single in Nashville. She was struggling with performance anxiety. A renowned Christian producer and a talented team were investing heavily in the project, and though she had sung the song hundreds of times, it felt stale and lifeless to her.

We prayed and asked God to breathe fresh life into the song. The Holy Spirit filled the room so profoundly that we were both in tears and wordless. A few weeks later, she went into the studio and nailed the recording. She told me she fell in love with the song all over again and felt God's presence so strongly that the session felt effortless. Her anxiety had turned to joy, and she was filled with peace and excitement. "God answered our prayer," she said. "He made the song new!"

These instances remind me what an honor it is to walk beside others as a kind of spiritual midwife—helping them give birth to the dreams God has placed inside them. And in cases like this, God bypasses various mechanisms—that all have their place—to do what only He can do. Ultimately, how encounters are facilitated does matter, but the encounter itself is what matters most.

CHAPTER ELEVEN
Dreams: Assembly Required

"Look, here comes that dreamer..." (Genesis 37:19)

As a child, dreams were a means of escape. As an adult, dreams have become an entryway. What started as maladaptive daydreaming—escaping reality for one I created—ended as *adaptive God-dreaming*—interpreting reality based on the one God was creating. So much of my life has been guided by dreams from God.

About fifteen years ago, while sitting under Dr. Corral, she held a series of Dream Activation Nights. We would bring our pillowcases in to be anointed and prayed over—which might sound unorthodox, but within days I started dreaming as never before. Since then, dreams have gone from being a fairly regular occurrence to being a constant part of my life, guiding me through decisions, warning me about obstacles, and confirming God's plans.

To ignore the reality of divine dreams is to undercut a huge method of communication from heaven. If God designed humans to spend a third of their lives sleeping, wouldn't it make sense that He would continue to engage with us during that slumber? The idea that the Holy Spirit would "tune out" at night doesn't align with how intimately God interacts with His people. Beyond that, it doesn't align with the Bible itself. Sleep is often when our minds are finally quiet enough for God to get through to us. When we are awake, our conscious minds can interfere with what God is trying to say. But when we sleep, our spirits remain active, and God can communicate without the static of daytime resistance.

The Bible speaks of dreams as one of the primary ways God communicates with His people: *"If there is a prophet among you, I, the Lord, make Myself known to him in a vision; I speak to him in a dream"* (Numbers 12:6).

This word for *vision* here is the Hebrew word *mar'eh*, which can actually mean glass (Strong's 4759). The word *dream* here is the word *chalom* (Strong's 2474), which means *window*. Think about going for a walk in your neighborhood, peering at the homes of your neighbors. Generally, you cannot see what's happening inside. However, if you look through a window or glass, you get a closer glimpse of things you normally would not be able to see. What God is saying in this passage is that when He gives a vision or dream, He is allowing us to peek into a matter we normally do not have access to.

God often chooses dreams as a medium of revelation. In my own life, dreams are one of the three primary ways I hear from God. They have been a guiding light, especially before major transitions or ministry assignments. Week by week, I receive insight through dreams—about people, about regions I'm ministering in, and sometimes about future events.

The truth is, dreams are not always crystal clear the minute you open your eyes in the morning. Often, your dreams come like an IKEA furniture box—there is assembly required. God gives you the pieces, but you have to put them together over time. You have fragments and puzzle pieces that require effort and discernment to properly put together. My goal with this chapter is to provide insight and practical wisdom on approaching, stewarding, and interpreting prophetic dreams with stories from my own journey accompanying the content.

But we've got to start with a basic qualifier: How can we tell the difference between a dream from God and a dream generated by our subconscious? We don't want to call a pizza dream prophetic, but we also don't want to dismiss a true prophetic dream as the byproduct of a late-night slice. This is a crucial area of this subject. Some dreams are simply reflections of our desires, fears, or recent circumstances. If you spend the day at a waterpark, you might dream about going down a water slide that night—that doesn't mean it's prophetic. For me, I always look for four key factors when discerning a dream's source:

1. Does it align with the Word of God? God will never contradict His nature or His truth.
2. Does it challenge me, or is it just convenient? God's voice isn't always comfortable. If a dream simply reinforces what I already want, I have to question whether it's truly from Him or just my subconscious.
3. Does the dream contain heavenly symbols? Many dreams from God contain heavenly symbols that we need to piece together, like a puzzle.
4. What is the fruit of the dream? If a dream brings wisdom, insight, or conviction, it's likely from God. If it causes fear, confusion, or self-exaltation, it's probably not.

David's prayer in Psalm 26:2 is a great model for this: *"Test me, Lord, and try me, examine my heart and my mind."* The Hebrew word for *"try me"* refers to the kidneys, which in biblical symbolism represent the filtering of toxins. When we evaluate our dreams, we have to ask: *Are my motives pure, or am I just seeing what I want to see?*

The last thing we want to do is misuse dreams to justify personal desires that weren't from God. Of course, all of this takes time to learn, experiment with, and test. Remember, we are chasing principles, not perfection. The Bible is the plumb line that helps us to navigate the dream-filled path ahead. As we do, I want to point to three *reasons* why dreams from God exist, and three methods for maximizing them.

1. PUZZLES

When God spoke of His relationship with Moses, He said, *"I speak to him face to face, not in dark speeches"* (Numbers 12:8). Interestingly, the Hebrew word translated as *"dark speeches"* means riddles or puzzles. This reveals something essential about dreams: sometimes God communicates with crystal-clear precision, while other times, He speaks through symbolic puzzles that must be unraveled. Speaking with riddles and puzzles was so normative that God had to make a point to distinguish the "face-to-face" chats that He had with Moses.

In the book of Job, we see a famous commentary on God dreams: *"For God may speak in one way, or in another, yet man does not perceive it. In a dream, in a vision of the night, when deep sleep falls upon men, while slumbering on their beds, then He opens the ears of men, and seals their instruction"* (Job 33:14–16). Too often, we overlook God's voice because we're expecting straightforward clarity when He deliberately chooses mystery. Dreams require us to go deeper, learning His unique language of symbols, metaphors, and riddles. This isn't God playing games with us; it's Him inviting us to intimacy.

Paul wrote, *"We know **in part**.... For now we see through a glass, darkly"* (1 Corinthians 13:9, 12). God's choice to speak through puzzles isn't meant to confuse or frustrate us. Instead, it's His way of drawing us closer, inviting us into the deeper waters of relationship. It's through the process of seeking, questioning, wrestling, and sometimes stumbling that we truly learn His character and ways.

We tend to value what we have to work for. If God's voice is *always* just a crystal clear, non-stop flow of obvious information, then we may not value His word when it comes to us. But when there is some assembly required, we will value, honor, and sustain that word. To all who dream, who seek clarity, and who wrestle with unanswered questions, know this: God isn't withholding clarity as a punishment. He's inviting you closer, one puzzle piece at a time, into deeper friendship and trust with Him.

2. TRUST BUILDING

God has often used dreams to teach me to trust that He has got my life figured out—sometimes in unexpected ways. One powerful example happened during a spontaneous trip to Portugal, just after COVID restrictions had eased. Visiting Lisbon had always been a dream of mine, and when an affordable flight popped up on my way home from a ministry trip in Egypt, I jumped at the chance to explore.

One afternoon, after exploring the beautiful coastal town of Cascais, the Holy Spirit whispered to me, "Take the train back." Initially, I brushed it off, figuring I'd stick with a familiar Uber. The next day, the whisper came back, stronger this time: "Take the train."

Sure enough, I found myself at the train station, struggling to sift through all of the unfamiliar routes. I was uneasy to say the least. Sitting on the train, a man sitting across from me began a conversation. With kindness and patience, he guided me through the complicated system. He had a reassuring spirit about him. I felt an overwhelming sense of comfort and safety, and enjoyed the process of navigating my way back to the hotel in the preferred transport of the locals.

That evening, I remembered my dream journal and felt compelled to search for the word "Portugal." I was astonished to rediscover a dream I'd had and written down two years earlier. In that dream, I had been in Portugal, hesitant and fearful of stepping into something unknown. Just as in my real-life experience, God had sent a man to comfort and guide me. The exact scene that had just played out on the train had played out in the night, 24 months before.

The truth is, after Priscilla tragically died, I became petrified and believed the lie that I was not safe. We trusted Priscilla's husband in our family and after she died by his hands, I believed a lie that I was not safe anymore. Through this experience in Portugal, God healed me of that lie once and for all. He challenged me thousands of miles away from my comfort zone, with no one to lean on but Him—and He came through. This encounter wasn't just about practical directions—it was a lesson where God was showing me I am safe, never alone, and every single detail of my life is orchestrated by Him and guided by His loving care. God's presence is not just about faith in an unseen force—but it is an experiential awareness, whether I am at home in the south, on a train in Lisbon, or in a plane above the Alps.

Dreams are not just black ink on a white page; they can become a living reality. Dreams aren't just glimpses into the future; they're invitations into deeper trust and closeness with God. Dreams don't have to be some wild, fine-tuned prediction. They can be a simple trust builder as you learn to hear God in the night seasons and to watch for the manifestations of those dreams in reality.

3. NOTIFICATIONS

We all need a heads-up sometimes—something that alerts us to what's coming down the pike. Dreams can act as spiritual notifications: guidance, direction, and divine reminders that help us prepare for what's ahead. They aren't just abstract symbols—they're part of God's way of equipping us for real, tangible events and decisions.

Joseph's dream in Genesis 41 is a classic example. God showed him that seven years of abundance would be followed by seven years of famine. That warning wasn't meant to induce fear, but to inspire strategy and preparation.

Because of that dream, Joseph was able to lead Egypt and many others through crisis. God's heart is so protective and forward-thinking—and dreams like this reveal that.

I've experienced these "notifications" firsthand. Before I ever joined Lance Wallnau's ministry, I had a vivid dream where I saw myself working alongside him. It was clear and specific. At the time, it felt far-fetched as I knew better to call him or his wife up and say, I'm supposed to work for you. Three months later, the opportunity opened up. Because of that dream, I wasn't confused or caught off guard when the call came—I was ready.

In January of 2020, I had a dream in which an angel handed me a pass to the White House. I had no connections and no expectations that anything of the sort was coming soon. But just days later, a friend called me: "We're having a private prayer meeting at the White House on January 5th, in Mike Pence's boardroom. Do you want to come?"

I was stunned—but not surprised. God had already sent the notification. He had gone ahead of me. Suddenly, I reflected on the text from my cousin a few years before: "God told me you're not moving to Raleigh for Raleigh. He's moving you there to get you closer to the White House." The word was confirmed by dream and made manifest in reality: I was in the White House in January to intercede for our nation and its leaders.

These divine notifications are part of how God prepares His people—not just for personal decisions, but for participation in the bigger story He's writing. When we pay attention, we're not just interpreting dreams; we're learning to move with Him.

Sometimes these notifications are an alert to something dangerous. Warnings are the kindness of God, calling us to avoid trouble. And ignoring those warnings can carry painful consequences. One of the hardest lessons I've learned came in 2011. I was sitting across from my sister Priscilla at lunch, listening as she spoke about her troubled marriage. Suddenly, I had a clear vision of her husband shooting her. But instead of heeding the vision, I brushed it off. I told myself, "You're just being morbid. This is just your imagination acting up because you're still grieving your brother."

Three months later, it happened—exactly as I had seen.

The grief was unbearable—but so was the realization that God had warned me, and I had brushed it off. It took years of inner healing to work through the guilt, but that moment forever changed the way I view dreams and visions. I learned that when God gives you a warning, you must pay attention and act accordingly. That warning should become a prayer assignment and a call to action.

Since then, I've received other warnings in dreams. Once, I had a dream about a church where dog excrement was on the floor—odd, yes, but symbolic. I knew it represented offense and bitterness festering in the atmosphere. I dismissed it at the time, not understanding the imagery. But weeks later, I found myself caught up in church drama I could have avoided had I recognized what God was trying to show me.

In another instance, while attending a church, I saw a vision of a rainbow hovering over a leader's head. Biblically, a rainbow is a symbol of God's covenant. But in this context, it had a different meaning. God was showing me that she was living a hidden lifestyle—a same-sex relationship. Being green in the understanding of visions, I innocently shared the vision with her, hoping it would encourage her, but she lashed out at me. The persecution that followed was intense.

There are people in this world who are called to steward finances, protect investments, or build businesses. And then there are those who are called to something far heavier—life and death. I've come to understand that my calling isn't just about helping people heal; it's about warning them, standing in the gap, and sometimes carrying the weight of seeing what they refuse to see.

Accepting this allowed me to not only plan for the future but to reinterpret my past. God revealed to me that my family was under the influence of the Jezebel spirit. It was like being hit over the head. It was undeniable, and I saw the impact of this influence everywhere, in the patterns of destruction, the deaths, and the generational strongholds. The losses were caused by the Jezebel spirit being tolerated and permitted to operate (see Revelation 2).

Having the prophetic insight and warnings available to see these things has positioned me to fight, to reclaim territory, and to partner with heaven to rewrite the destiny of me and my family.

* * *

Knowing *why* God gives us dreams is great. Knowing what to do with them is even better. Once we understand the purpose of our dreams, the next step is learning how to carefully steward them. Here are three simple practices that help us respond well to the dreams God gives.

1. WRITE THEM DOWN

I have been asked, "Do you keep a dream journal?" The answer is a wholehearted *yes*. And I recommend you do the same. God said, *"Write the vision and make it plain on tablets, that he may run who reads it"* (Habakkuk 2:2). To run with a vision, we've got to see the vision, and often that means seeing it clearly on a page. A journal will also help you track recurring patterns and themes over time.

In today's digital age, I've found the Notes app to be useful. As of today, when I search the word *dream*, I have over 750 documents in my phone that populate, all detailing the various dreams God has given me.

From whom to partner with in ministry to how to navigate a complicated organizational situation, to warnings about future spiritual attacks. I have a stockpile of dreams that act as an insight database, helping me navigate the road ahead. Writing down dreams has been one of the most life-giving habits I've developed. It allows me to go back and trace patterns—connections I might have missed initially but become clear over time. Some dreams make sense immediately; others are pieces of a larger puzzle that only fit together months or even years later. Without a dream journal, it would be difficult or impossible to finish gathering all the pieces needed.

I always encourage people to write their dreams down right away—ideally, as soon as you wake up. As we transition from the dream world into waking life, the clarity can begin to fade. The longer we wait, the more details we lose. But if we capture them quickly, those fragments often become the breadcrumbs that lead us into deeper insight.

God doesn't waste His words. If He's speaking through dreams, then we should treat them like treasures—recorded, revisited, and reflected upon. Because sometimes the key to today's breakthrough is hidden in a dream from last year.

2. STUDY SYMBOLS

If you don't understand biblical symbols, dreams can feel frustrating. I was coaching a client recently who had several dreams full of symbols she didn't understand. We sat down with *The Divinity Code* by Adrian Beale and Adam Thompson—one of my favorite dream interpretation books—and worked through each symbol. By the end, a stronghold in her life was exposed. The dream was revealing not only the problem but also the solution.

In modern Western cultures, we've lost sight of the value of symbols. Thinking symbolically does not come naturally. We live in a post-printing press world where everything is written down directly and literally. However, in ancient Near Eastern history, symbols were everything. Imagery, metaphor, and layered meaning were the ways that truth was communicated and passed down. Understanding biblical symbolism brings clarity where there was once confusion.

This idea of symbolic language is also found in Scripture. Take Pharaoh's dream in Genesis 41. Without Joseph's help, Pharaoh might have dismissed the dream about fat and skinny cows as nonsense. But Joseph was grounded in the language of God and recognized it as a divine warning and forecast. That insight didn't just inform Pharaoh—it saved a nation.

In Matthew, the wise men were warned in a dream not to return to Herod. In Daniel, King Nebuchadnezzar had symbol-filled dreams that prophesied future world empires. The truth is, if we want to grow in our ability to hear God through dreams, we must become students of the language He speaks. That means leaning into Scripture, studying symbolism, numbers, and asking the Holy Spirit for interpretation. When we do, the hidden becomes revealed—and what once seemed confusing starts to make sense.

DREAMS: ASSEMBLY REQUIRED

Context also matters deeply. A symbol doesn't carry the same meaning in every situation. I shared earlier about a dream involving a rainbow over a lady. Traditionally, a rainbow represents God's promise, like in the story of Noah. But in some cases, the rainbow might reveal a hidden compromise in someone's life. Symbols have to be interpreted through the lens of *context*, wisdom, and the Holy Spirit's guidance.

When interpreting dreams, it's a hybrid of spiritual discernment and knowledge of biblical symbols. Some symbols are so recurring and clear that it doesn't take a deep level of discernment to grasp the meaning. For instance, if I'm driving a vehicle in a dream, it usually represents a ministry or calling. The bigger the vehicle, the heavier the assignment. When I worked at Elijah List, I had recurring dreams about a huge airplane—because the ministry was heavy-duty. After transitioning to Lance Wallnau's ministry, I noticed a shift in my dreams. I began dreaming of being mid-flight, symbolizing the momentum and altitude of his ministry's work.

Before I travel to minister in a city, I often have dreams revealing the region's spiritual climate. If I see an alligator in a dream, for example, I know it often symbolizes pride. That's my signal to prepare in humility and walk in the opposite spirit when I arrive. I've had dreams where I was kissing someone—not romantically, but because the act of kissing in dreams often symbolizes agreement, I know there is an alignment in motion.

If an object, a number, or a place in a dream strikes you as odd or unusual, let me encourage you to look into the possible symbolism. Research instances in the Bible where that sort of thing has shown up. Refer to balanced, biblical books like *The Divinity Code* as resources for learning as well. We owe it to ourselves and to our walk with God to gain clarity in this area.

If you are in America, you probably speak English. If you are in Germany, you speak German. If you are in Spain, you speak Spanish. Similarly, if you are in a dream from God, you likely speak the language of symbols. Learn the language and enjoy the fruit that it brings!

3. FIND A SOUNDING BOARD

Once you've written your dreams down and studied their symbols, the next vital step is to find a trusted sounding board. This is particularly important as you're starting out. Dreams often carry layers of meaning, and even the most spiritually mature can sometimes benefit from godly counsel when trying to interpret them. We were never meant to discern everything in isolation.

When King Nebuchadnezzar had troubling dreams, he turned to Daniel for interpretation. Daniel didn't rely on his own wisdom—he sought God's understanding and delivered a message that changed the course of history. The takeaway? Interpretation isn't just about insight—it's about partnership with the Holy Spirit and, often, with wise people around us.

Never underestimate the power of a third-party. Christianity and Spirit-led living are not an event between a person and God—it's a person and God *in community*. Surround yourself with people who value dreams and can help interpret them wisely—leaders who have a strong, stable background.

Having a sounding board can save you from unnecessary confusion or even heartache. Without guidance, it's easy to misread symbols or project our meaning onto what God is saying. Take something like dirty water. On its own, that might not seem significant. But biblically, murky water usually represents strife, confusion, or deception. Even muddying the flow of God's Spirit. God will use plays on words, metaphors, and emotional impressions that need to be unpacked—often in the presence of a trusted person.

But here's the key: fruit matters. Don't just share your dreams with anyone. Find people who have a proven track record of hearing from God and walking in wisdom. Otherwise, you risk receiving poor advice that may cloud your discernment instead of sharpening it. Dreams are more than just spiritual mysteries—they're road maps to our destiny. But even the best map is hard to follow alone. When we learn to walk with others in this journey, our clarity grows, our discernment sharpens, and our confidence deepens.

WHAT KIND IS IT?

Throughout our lives—and certainly throughout Scripture—we see that not all dreams are created equal. Some carry divine messages; others reflect our inner life; and others are spiritual warfare in disguise. It's not just about having a dream—it's about discerning the *kind* of dream it is. That's what determines whether we partner with the dream in faith or dismiss it as noise.

Learning to ask, "What kind of dream is this?" can turn a fleeting nighttime vision into a lasting breakthrough. In the section to follow, I want to provide some categories for you to consider, along with explanations, as you journey in dreams.

Time Marker Dreams

These are like little road signs along the path of your journey. God gives you a dream not necessarily to do something with, but to let you know where you are—to mark a moment and whisper, "You're on track. Don't give up." These dreams bring encouragement and perspective when you're deep in the wait or wondering if you've missed something.

There have been times when the dream didn't seem significant, but viewing it later helped me see that God had already been preparing my heart for something long before it showed up in the natural. These dreams are God's gentle way of saying, "I see you. Keep going."

In 2021, God gave me a dream that President Donald Trump would return to the White House as President. In the dream, everyone thought he was finished and would never come back. In my circle, many people had given up and believed the days of his presidency were over. Some even labeled those who prophesied his return as *radical*. God gave me this dream to show that, although many believed he would serve two *consecutive* terms, he would, in fact, have a second term — just not consecutively.

Warning Dreams

These are not "bad dreams"—they're merciful ones. God loves us enough to give us a heads-up. Warning dreams are often vivid and emotionally charged, designed to shake us awake—literally and spiritually.

Think of Joseph being told to flee with Mary and baby Jesus. (See Matthew 2:13.) That dream saved their lives. I've had dreams that warned me of relationships, decisions, or spiritual traps I didn't yet see in the natural.

The night before an out-of-state ministry meeting, I had a dream in which a terrorist was planting bombs beneath each window of the building, attempting to sabotage the gathering. He moved methodically from window to window, placing explosives intended to cause disruption and chaos. In the dream, I called the authorities before waking up. Immediately afterward, I alerted the Here Comes Joy prayer team so they could intercede and break potential distractions.

During the actual ministry meeting, as we prayed for people, numerous disruptions arose, drawing attention away from Jesus and toward a particular individual. These interruptions hindered the flow of the Spirit, as the anointing would lift. Despite the challenge, we pressed on—and

God moved powerfully, bringing healing and deliverance to countless lives.

The dream also served as confirmation that God was with us and fully aware of what was truly taking place. This reduces the confusion amid warfare, so you can keep your focus on Jesus.

When you receive a warning dream, don't panic—pray. Ask the Lord for clarity, protection, and wisdom. The purpose isn't fear, but safety—so you can stay aligned with God's plan for your life.

Prophetic Dreams

These are the dreams that leave you wide-eyed and wondering. They often reveal glimpses of God's plans, future events, or personal destiny. Just like Joseph's dreams of ruling over his brothers (see Genesis 37), prophetic dreams may not make sense right away—and not everyone will celebrate them.

But that doesn't mean they're not from God. Write them down. Pray over them. Don't force them into action prematurely. Prophetic dreams are seeds—they grow in the right time and soil.

Direction Dreams

Ever felt stuck between two options and then had a dream that pointed the way? That's what a direction dream does—it brings clarity.

Think of Paul's dream in Acts 16, where a man from Macedonia says, "Come help us." That one dream altered the course of his missionary journey and changed history.

God still gives dreams like that today. If you're discerning a decision and you receive a dream that brings peace and clarity, don't ignore it. God's voice is not limited to waking hours.

Encouragement Dreams

These dreams are akin to a warm blanket from the Holy Spirit. They may not be loud or dramatic, but they leave you comforted, seen, and strengthened.

Remember Gideon in Judges 7? He was hiding, afraid, and overwhelmed. Then he overheard a Midianite's dream that confirmed God's plan for victory. It gave him the courage to step into his assignment.

God still uses dreams to build us up—especially when we're weary or discouraged. They remind us, "I'm with you. I'm for you. Keep going."

Self-Condition Dreams

These are the mirrors of the night. They don't always feel spiritual, but they're deeply revealing. God uses them to show us what's going on inside—fears we haven't named, pride we haven't addressed, wounds we haven't let Him touch.

Nebuchadnezzar's dream in Daniel 4 exposed his arrogance and warned him of the fall that would come unless he repented. These dreams can feel uncomfortable, but they are invitations to deeper healing and maturity.

Don't brush them off. Bring them to the Lord and ask, "What are You trying to show me about myself?"

Calling Dreams

These dreams mark you. They affirm your identity and reveal the purpose God has woven into your life.

Samuel heard God calling him in the night (see 1 Samuel 3), and though he didn't recognize the voice at first, it was the beginning of his prophetic journey. These dreams might not come often, but when they do, they tend to stick with you.

Some time ago, a significant shift occurred in ministry. Before this, I had a dream where I was flying with the

Here Comes Joy team in a plane, flying low to the ground through hostile territory. We were on healing missions for the Lord.

The hostile territory represented spiritually resistant environments—places marked by demonic opposition or human resistance. The dream served as a prophetic glimpse into the season we were entering. During those meetings, God moved powerfully, bringing healing and deliverance to individuals carrying decades of pain and wounding.

Through this dream, the Lord was revealing that close, personal healing assignments—those "low to the ground"—often come with intense spiritual resistance. These missions require more than just discernment and authority; they demand prayer, deep humility, and a willingness to die to self to be vessels God can fully work through.

If you've had a dream that resonates with your core identity or assignment, take it seriously. God is confirming who you are—and who you're becoming.

Healing and Deliverance Dreams

God doesn't wait until daylight to heal us. I've had people tell me they woke up feeling lighter, freer, or deeply moved—like something shifted overnight.

Sometimes in a dream, you'll revisit a traumatic moment, but this time, Jesus is there. Or you'll feel chains breaking or rooms being cleared. These are not just emotional—they're spiritual.

Dreams can be a place where God reaches into the deepest parts of us and brings freedom we didn't even know we needed. Wake up and give thanks—something sacred happened while you slept.

Soul Dreams

Not every dream is divine. Sometimes, it's just your soul sorting through life. These dreams tend to echo your own thoughts, worries, or desires. They aren't bad—they're just you.

They can still be helpful, though. If you're always dreaming of being late, chased, or stuck, your inner world might be trying to tell you something. Soul dreams can reveal what your heart is carrying—and what needs to be surrendered. The more you learn to recognize them, the easier it is to discern when God isn't speaking—so you don't misinterpret something He didn't say.

Demonic Dreams

Yes, the enemy speaks in dreams, too. These dreams usually carry fear, confusion, heaviness, or seduction. They're meant to intimidate, torment, or distract.

But don't let them scare you—let them wake you up. When you have a demonic dream, it's often a sign to go deeper in prayer, shut open doors, or break agreement with something that has gained access.

Put on the armor of God (see Ephesians 6), plead the blood of Jesus over your sleep, and remember: you have authority. Don't partner with the darkness—stand in the light.

* * *

If we believe the world is getting darker, then we need to be hearing from God more clearly than ever. Dreams are more than a boost to the Christian life—they are often the very means by which God delivers the gospel. In many places around the world—like China, North Korea, and Iran—people are experiencing dreams and visions of Jesus and coming to faith. There are testimonies upon testimonies of Christians in persecuted nations receiving dreams that literally save their lives. God will warn them, "Get out of this building now; leave the city," and so forth.

We may not be at that level of persecution in the West, but why wait until we are desperate to develop our sensitivity to the Holy Spirit? Now is the time for the body of Christ to train ourselves to listen in the night just as carefully as we do in the day. The next generations must be equipped to hear from God through dreams, because there will come a time when it will be imperative. We are already living in an era where deception is rampant. How much more will we need discernment in the days ahead?

Dreams are no small matter. Dreams often reveal things that are too big for us to comprehend at the time. If your dreams are bigger than you, then you are dreaming in the right direction. God often gives us dreams that feel impossible to remind us that He is the only one who can bring them to pass.

Six years ago, I had one of the most profound dreams of my life. In the dream, I was at the White House on assignment, and a man was there with me. I hadn't met him yet in real life, but I could see him. He was African American, and he had such a kind and loving spirit. In the dream, I recall watching him sleep, feeling so deeply in love and at peace. But what stood out to me most was the realization that I didn't yet have the capacity to love someone so purely with such abandon. I was still on a healing journey, and I woke up excited about the possibility and thinking, *That level of love and surrender is foreign to me.*

God wasn't just showing me a man in my future—He was preparing my heart to love him unconditionally. The following five years contained some of the deepest healing imaginable, as written about prior. The man *in* my dream would become the man *of* my dreams. When the dream happened and my heart underwent a massive season of preparation, I realized this man was not just a piece of the future - he was already on his way into my life.

CHAPTER TWELVE

Now and Forever

"A threefold cord is not quickly broken." (Ecclesiastes 4:12)

Six years had passed since my dream. By then, I had been single for sixteen years when, in December of 2023, I received a prophetic word from a friend named Sandy Binder. We were on a call, praying, and she had a vision of me getting married. She said, "God is bringing you a Moses." She went on to explain that, much like a person we both knew, I would recognize in three weeks that this man was going to be my husband. She said, "It's going to happen fast!"

Then a month later, a close friend, Josh Gardner, was ministering prophetically at church, when he pointed at me and said, in front of the entire congregation, "Your wedding gown cometh quickly. You've been waiting and have been faithful; now your gown is coming."

After that, in April of 2024, yet another prophetic word came. I was visiting a dear friend, Sandi Jenkins, when—right in the middle of prayer—she looked at me and said, "I see you being married underneath a *tallit* (a Jewish prayer shawl), and by October of this year, your life is going to look completely different."

As if that weren't enough, another friend, Christy Allen, approached me after a ministry meeting and said, "When you were ministering earlier, I saw a vision of a handsome Black man standing beside you, wearing a blue suit."

The vision sounded incredible. I wanted to believe these words, but a small part of me was afraid—afraid of being disappointed.

In part, I was comfortable in my own space. If I didn't care for an environment or a person's attitude while out and about, I could just check out, leave, and retreat to my peaceful home by myself. Marriage would bring that sort of seclusion to a close, so God needed to alert me strongly ahead of time, and that He did.

After years of surrender, of healing, and of letting go of what I thought life would look like, I had truly laid marriage down at the feet of Jesus. Not out of any sort of disillusionment, but surrender. I wasn't trying to make anything happen.

Yet, God had already begun orchestrating the connection between Jarrett and me, using someone very dear to both of us—Dr. Alveda King, Jarrett's mother. One day, she called him and said, "I have a favor to ask — and you can't say no!" We still get a kick out of her determination to this day and are so grateful. She continued, "There's someone I want you to meet. I believe this is from God. She walks in the Kingdom, and I think she would be a good person for you to know. Would you be open to being interviewed on her podcast?"

She had been praying about introducing us for some time before finally moving forward. By then, Jarrett was in the same place I was—having prayed prayers like, "Lord, I don't want to date anymore. If this is going to happen, You'll have to bring the right person to me."

We had both reached a point of surrender, fully aware that unless the Lord built it, we weren't interested. Jarrett had already decided he wouldn't entertain any more set-ups. He sensed that his mother secretly hoped that this would be more than a meeting of new friends, and he was prepared to decline her request. But as she spoke, the Holy Spirit whispered, "This is a call you want to take."

Before my first phone call with Jarrett, I had finished up an inner healing session. I was saying a cleansing prayer in preparation to have a clear head and spirit for my call with him. As I prayed, I *audibly* heard a man speaking. It was a tender, kind, comforting voice. Little did I know it was Jarrett's voice, which was confirmed shortly after when I got on the line with him. Never has anything like that happened to me before—God had given me a recognition of his voice before we ever connected, an imprint of the man he is upon my heart. Jarrett later told me that he had a similar experience as he watched an interview of me online before we spoke. He felt that in hearing my voice in that interview, he knew something meaningful about my heart, that I championed others, perhaps more than I championed myself. He felt his own heart rise to be my champion as a friend, thinking it was too much to hope for more. We chuckle today, realizing that he didn't have the benefit of the four different prophetic voices who had provided such eagle-eye confirmation for me within six months.

We began with that simple phone call, but hours in, it became clear that something more was happening, a powerful wave in the spirit; a connection that neither of us could explain nor find the words for. There was a weight to the conversation, yet a lightness too—as though we were being drawn to something life-giving and important. It felt like the deep had called to the deep.

Similarly, Jarrett later told me he had also received a dream before we met about his future spouse. The Holy Spirit powerfully recalled it for him during our honeymoon. Clearly, this was God's doing and not an event of our own making.

Our conversations continued daily with a depth and joy that neither of us had ever known before romantically. We shared our hearts openly without reservation or fear. There was a sense of safety in each other's presence, both of us. We experienced a closeness in each conversation, discussing our deepest hopes and beliefs

He was in Atlanta and I was in Raleigh, so we made plans to meet. The richness of our conversations multiplied in person. Our engagement came quickly, not because we rushed, but because the Lord went before us in every detail. When you know, *you know*. God had already been preparing us—softening our hearts, healing our wounds, and aligning our paths. He was writing a love story we couldn't have come up with on our own.

Like Rebekah at the well, God brought me to the place where my husband would find me—not by striving, but by the Spirit. We were surrounded by people who didn't just have good intentions, but who had discernment and grace for timing. The grace of God makes all the difference. Anyone and everyone can come up with decent advice to give those who are single. But the question has to be: Is God in it? With Jarrett, God was not just part of the equation, but He was the very author of the entire connection.

From the start, I could see Jarrett carried a mercy gift. He has this quiet strength, this justice in his heart. He comes from a family legacy of civil rights—being the great-nephew of Dr. Martin Luther King Jr. Healing and reconciliation flow out of him. I instantly recognized our similarities, given my role in inner healing and reconciliation in a ministry capacity. He is an incredible attorney who also enters the courts of heaven in prayer and intercession. Likewise, I operate in the courts of heaven as an intercessor. There was alignment from day one.

While we were dating, Alveda traveled to North Carolina with Jarrett. Months earlier, we had planned a ministry weekend that included visits to several churches—and inviting Jarrett became the perfect excuse to bring him out to see me. Both Alveda and I were excited about the opportunity. One of our stops was Living Waters Church in Durham—which just so happens to be Christy Allen's church.

Jarrett arrived wearing a blue suit—just as Christy had prophesied only weeks earlier. She came up to me, pointed out the handsome Black man in the blue suit, and we both smiled, celebrating the goodness and faithfulness of God. At the time, that blue suit happened to be Jarrett's go-to for formal occasions.

At one dinner, Alveda—picking up on the chemistry between us and how happy we were—turned to Jarrett and asked, "So, are you planning to get her a ring?" Without missing a beat, he replied, "I've already been thinking about rings."

I was elated. Deep in my heart, I knew—this was it. This was the man God had been preparing me for over the past year.

The thing about my life is that I had gotten used to flying by the seat of my pants. I rarely knew what to expect, but somehow I always managed to land on my feet. I thrived on the challenge—winging it felt like an adventure. God knew that about me. And He also knew how much preparation it would take to merge two lives, especially after years of living independently.

Months before Jarrett even showed up in my life, I started preparing my home. I cleaned out the pantry, bedrooms, and closets—anything I no longer used, I gave away. I even hired a crew to tackle the garage. Physically, my house was ready. But emotionally? Spiritually? I wasn't sure how to prepare to share my space, my rhythm, and my life with someone after being single for 17 years.

The one thing I was sure of was that God was in this with me. And for everything I didn't know how to prepare for, I'd have to trust Him. In every part of this new season, God's presence wasn't optional—it was essential. Without Him, I knew I'd be sunk.

During our brief engagement, I hopped on a Zoom call with a friend, Josh Gardner, who was seeking guidance on inner healing for his daughter. Usually, I'm the one doing the praying and ministering on these calls. What Josh didn't know was that I was privately wrestling with doubts about how fast things were moving toward marriage.

As the call wrapped up, Josh began to revisit a vision he'd had more than seven months earlier, when he prophesied about my gown. Something about the way he shifted caught my attention, so I hit the record button. Then he began:

This time, I saw the white wedding gown on you. I saw combat boots underneath it, and I also saw a scepter in your hand. I heard the Spirit of God say, 'You can have both a gown and a scepter. Just because you wear a gown doesn't mean you lose your scepter. You'll walk in a wedding dress, but your feet will be in combat boots. It may look like you're walking into a battle, but you'll carry the authority to legislate in your hand. You are a bride of war and legislation, my daughter.' Your dress completely covers the boots—God will cover the war going on underneath. The scepter you carry is embedded with all twelve gemstones of the ephod. The gown He's placed on you doesn't strip you of your independence. You may feel the urge to run because you're afraid this will cost you your freedom or your calling. But He says you won't lose it. You don't have to choose between the gown and the scepter. You get to keep both.

His word lasted about fifteen minutes—but every second hit home. Josh spoke straight to the core of what I was wrestling with. I hadn't shared any of my fears with anyone, and yet here he was, describing them in detail. As he spoke, I felt the word of the Lord wash over me. Healing came. Peace came. And I knew—*I really knew*—that everything was going to be okay. That word set me free from the fear of losing my independence.

I approached the wedding with full assurance that God was gracing each step to the altar, and each step Jarrett and I would take afterward.

By then, Rachel had become a successful doctor. She and I had spent our entire adult lives sending each other clothes and gifts—and when the time came, she stepped up and practically paid for the entire wedding. She spared no expense! The trauma of neglect and poverty resulted in us both being very generous with resources, and she certainly demonstrated that for our wedding.

Jarrett and I walked the aisle in June of 2024, and Alveda officiated.

In addition, we planned to visit Dr. Corral's church in California on Rosh Hashanah of that same year. She agreed to officiate a second ceremony for our family in the area who couldn't make it to the Atlanta wedding. Because of the timing, without planning it, we ended up wearing Prayer Shawls or talits during the wedding service—exactly as Sandi Jenkins had prophesied months before.

And as if that weren't enough confirmation, another divine connection emerged. Dr. Corral already had long-standing friendships with Dr. Bernice King—Jarrett's cousin—and with Coretta Scott King, the widow of Dr. Martin Luther King Jr. You can't make this stuff up. It was another elliptical thread in a story God had been weaving for generations.

Jarret and I wasted no time flowing in the Spirit together, discovering that we carried a breaker anointing. Together, we've prayed over people, seen miracles break out, led meetings and programs, and watched God break chains that some felt could not be broken. Beyond a love story, my marriage is a story of Kingdom connection and synergy in the Spirit.

We know that the three-fold cord represents a husband, wife, and God all united together. When one is weary, the other stands. When one is uncertain, the other holds faith. But the picture of a cord in Ecclesiastes is more than a simple analogy. In ancient history, cords mattered far more than they might today. These woven ropes would have been used for transport, construction, measurement, tent-making, fishing, and more. They were not peripheral to society but *central* to a society's infrastructure. Likewise, when united as a husband and wife to the Lord, we become central to holding society together. Ropes bind, secure, and uphold in the same way that godly marriage binds together, secures, and upholds a society.

Jarrett has talked about once believing that marriage was more of a reward from God. If we stay faithful and petition Him, He will grant it as He chooses. But he has now seen that God proactively institutes marriage—it's His invention. It's not a reward for serving God but a central covenant to God's plan on earth.

While Jarrett had to unlearn the idea of marriage as a reward, I had to unlearn the idea of marriage as a hindrance. Before meeting Jarrett, I felt concerned that marriage was not in the cards because of the ministry God had called me to. Prophet Sharon Stone had said to me, "So many people have told you to dumb it down. That you can't be a powerful woman in ministry and still find love. That you can't be a powerful woman without threatening others. I destroy that lie off of you."

That lie had held me captive for so long, but when she spoke those words, it was as if a veil lifted. I didn't have to fit into a box to be loved or accepted. I could be fully myself, the woman God created me to be, flourishing in the ministry He gave me. God was able to make a match where our ministries did not conflict but complemented each other. Married couples have an incredible level of spiritual authority, but many don't tap into it.

The Scriptures make it clear: *"One can chase a thousand, but two can put ten thousand to flight"* (Deuteronomy 32:30). The enemy wants to keep husbands and wives too busy, distracted, or divided to pray together, because he knows how powerful their agreement in prayer can be. Jarrett and

I have stayed committed to using the connection God has given us as an entry point for heaven to invade earth—it's a role we don't take lightly.

After our wedding, I began transitioning my life from North Carolina to Georgia, but even in that natural move, I knew it was more than a change in scenery. Jarrett and I were merging households, callings, mandates, and assignments. Together, we are preparing for future assignments that will require both of us—spiritually, strategically, and prophetically. Whether in the church, government, media, or any other mountain, our matrimony is a mandate to see the Kingdom established on earth.

* * *

God doesn't always wait for perfection—He works through process. When He brought Jarrett into my life, it wasn't because we were both perfectly healed, but because we were ready enough to grow together. Sometimes, answered prayer appears as companionship in the healing, not completion before the journey begins. Because our engagement and marriage happened so suddenly, one thing we intentionally agreed on was to prioritize inner healing—however that might look—at least once each quarter during our first year or two together. As we merged our lives, we wanted to stay attentive to our individual growth and emotional health. Jarrett felt especially good about this commitment, having walked through a difficult journey before we met. We learned many lessons through trial and error during our first year of marriage. Still, God was undeniably faithful as we began to merge our lives.

Our first ministry engagement as a married couple was in St. Simons Island, Georgia. Because travel was already a frequent part of our lives, we had agreed early on to stay together during the first year of marriage, even while traveling—and this trip was no exception.

Leading up to it, we spent time in prayer together. Each time we prayed, the presence of God would meet us—His glory would fill the room. It was such strong confirmation that God was all over our union. When we arrived at the retreat, ministry flowed so naturally. We literally took turns ministering, walking hand-in-hand around the room, praying for people. The glory of God was tangible, and His Spirit moved powerfully. People were touched, healed, and deeply ministered to.

In the days following, we began receiving testimonies—stories of breakthrough, situations that had been stuck suddenly shifting. Over and over, we heard that attendees had never seen anything like this, a couple flowing seamlessly in ministry together, hand-in-hand in body and spirit, the Holy Spirit moving through husband and wife as one. It was exciting, humbling, and deeply affirming. That milestone marked not just the beginning of our marriage but the merging of our callings—and God was right at the center of it all.

The pattern has continued. In each of the last three ministry meetings, from California to North Carolina, Jarrett and I stayed behind to minister one-on-one after the services. One meeting went until 11:30 pm. Every time, we saw God move in a deeply personal way. At least a dozen or more people were healed at each gathering, simply through the act of holding and hugging them. Most were women, and within ten to twenty minutes—through tears, releasing loss, pain, trauma—many were delivered from deep wounds, emotional strongholds, and years of being stuck. We barely spoke; God's love did the work. It was raw, holy, and profoundly beautiful.

As soon as our ministry together began, we noticed something new. Entering our honeymoon, I shared with Jarrett that I felt that God was giving a special grace and peace before calling us back into the field. When we returned to action in St. Simons Island, we experienced a heavy spiritual attack, backlash from the enemy for ministering God's grace. We sought God's face for keys to overcome, as well as Dr. Michelle Corral, who had now become our spiritual mother. We learned to guard our hearts in some of our extended relationships. Over the next nine months or so, we allowed God to redefine our boundaries as a couple, and doing so significantly reduced the warfare we had been experiencing. We learned, sometimes the hard way, not to share personal details with people who are constantly stirring the pot or "burning up the phone lines" with worldly distractions.

One of the most expensive lessons I've learned is the value of peace. Peace has a price—but it's worth paying. A life marked by peace is one that God blesses, because He doesn't partner with chaos. His presence doesn't dwell where there is strife or demonic drama. And if someone isn't willing to pay the price to live in peace, they shouldn't be allowed a front-row seat to your life.

Similarly, not everyone has paid the price it takes to carry the presence of God. It requires inner work that costs something: time in the Word, sacrificial time in God's presence, financial investments in healing and coaching, and deep personal surrender. If someone isn't willing to confront darkness, kick the enemy out of their life, or die to self, they're not ready for close access to yours.

These are lessons we didn't learn lightly—but we learned them for life. Today, we choose to love broadly, but build boundaries wisely. Just as we work out our salvation with fear and trembling, we've learned to guard our peace, steward our union, and walk out our marriage with the kind of wisdom only God can give.

Not everyone gets access to the holy ground God has built between us.

After 17 years of divorce, God brought the most incredible man into my life—someone through whom He has healed and redeemed many broken places in both of our pasts. This love is sacred, and it's worth protecting. We both know that our only hope for lasting joy and success is to keep God at the center of our marriage, putting Him first in everything we do. As with every other part of our lives, when we surrender it all to Christ, He makes it whole— more beautiful than we ever imagined.

In so many ways, this season feels like a quiet reward... not a finish line, but a continuation. A redemptive chapter written in soft strokes, not sharp turns. I no longer strive to be perfect, but to be present. I no longer live to prove something, but to live out the story God has entrusted to me with grace, with joy, and with a heart wide open.

HERE COMES JOY

As I reflect on where I've been and where I'm going, this poem that I shared with Jarrett while we were dating captures it perfectly:

I want to age like sea glass.
Smoothed by tides
but not broken.
I want my hard edges to soften.
I want to ride the waves
and go with the flow.
I want to catch a wave
and let it carry me
to where I belong.
I want to be picked up
and held gently by
those who delight in my
well-earned patina and
appreciate the changes I went
through to achieve that beauty.
I want to enjoy the journey
and always remember that if
you give the ocean something
breakable, it will turn it into
something beautiful.
I want to age like sea glass.

— Bernadette Noll

And maybe that's the point. Not to avoid the process God has chosen, but to trust that every crashing wave, every tumbling current, is being used by God to shape us into something beautiful. Something enduring. My story isn't polished and perfect; it's softened, surrendered, and still unfolding. And I wouldn't have it any other way.

* * *

I haven't always understood why God chooses to conceal certain chapters of a person's past from memory until later in life—but I'm grateful He did in my case. As the layers of my heart began to peel back, I found myself becoming more whole—more rooted in my identity, and more certain of who I truly am in Christ; however, I still sensed there was more.

One night before Jarrett and I were scheduled to leave for a ministry trip, I felt the Lord drawing me to spend time in His presence. Jarrett joined, and I'm so thankful he did. As I settled into stillness, a new fragment of memory surfaced from the long-buried summer in Arkansas where my mother used to send me to visit my grandfather when I was a child. As I alluded in Chapter One, something was amiss and I would soon realize that one particular visit set a pattern of trauma that would haunt me from that time until now. I must have been around five years old. As I leaned into the Holy Spirit a bit further, I saw an image—a man carrying me into the woods. I didn't see any more at that moment, but a sudden, suffocating wave of shame flooded over me. I knew this wasn't imagined. My spirit remembered what my mind had been protecting me from for decades.

Instinctively, I began praying for that little girl, asking God to hold her, to heal her. But the shame was nearly unbearable. I broke into sobs—deep, guttural weeping that I could hardly control. Jarrett wrapped his arms around me and held me as I sobbed. My mind didn't have the full picture yet, but my heart was grieving as if it did. And in the weeks that followed, the shock would deepen.

By that time, Jarrett and I had been studying under Paul Cox, a deeply humble and Spirit-filled man known for his work in inner healing and deliverance. Paul, now in his eighties, once told us that the most profound healing of his life had taken place in just the last two years. That humbled us and gave us hope—because healing has no age limit in the Kingdom of God. Paul graciously referred us to his ministry network, and during one of those sessions, everything shifted.

Following a strong prompting from the Holy Spirit, I felt led to renounce generational ties to Freemasonry and the Scottish Rite on my mom's side. I knew my grandfather had been involved, but I didn't know to what extent. He had always been reclusive and secretive. Jarrett prayed a renunciation prayer written by Paul Cox aloud on my behalf—I didn't have the strength to speak it myself. When it was finished, I could hardly stand. The deliverance was deep, holy, and utterly exhausting.

I remained in bed for two days—grieving and resting. During that time, more pieces of memory began to surface. I saw my grandfather, peering down at me, surrounded by spiritual darkness. From the perspective of that little girl, he was terrifying.

A week later, I met with a spirit-led therapist and dear friend of Paul's, who walks in both gentleness and great spiritual authority. She encouraged me to revisit the memory, reminding me that all the Holy Spirit needs is a single fragment to bring more healing.

As she prayed, the memory unfolded. This time, I saw myself lying on a table in the woods, surrounded by people. It was mercifully veiled, protected by the Holy Spirit—but I could feel the horror. I began to weep again. The defilement, the betrayal, the deep humiliation—it all poured out. My therapist interceded as I grieved for the little girl who had endured the unimaginable.

And then came something I hadn't expected: anger. A holy, righteous anger rose up in me as I sat with the question: How could someone do this to a little girl?

It wasn't a rage that consumed me—it was a cry for justice, for truth, for the wrong to be named and condemned. Since we're made in the image of God, we're given a full gamut of emotions just as God has, and anger is one of them. The Bible says in Ephesians 4:26 be angry, but sin not.

I therefore had to allow myself to feel that anger, to process it, to grieve not only what had been done to me, but the cruelty and evil behind it. Suppressing it wouldn't heal me—but surrendering it to Jesus would.

For a brief moment, I saw myself—that helpless little girl—trapped in a cage. It was a vision of my subconscious, fragmented and frozen in time. That little girl had been locked away for decades, waiting for freedom to find her... waiting for Jesus to come with truth, comfort and healing. And He did. It would take weeks to grieve and release this painful chapter of my childhood. As the Lord led, I'd cry while driving, while sitting at the dinner table or lying in bed.

As I write this, my heart still grieves the years lost and the innocence stolen. But I can now rejoice—because that little girl is no longer locked away in captivity. She is no longer afraid. She is no longer bound.

She is free. She is seen. She is safe.

I write this part of my story, which is extremely vulnerable and challenging, for all those who have been hurt by abuse, in whatever form. I write for those who, through trauma, were locked away, unseen. I write for those who had no voice to shout, "NO!" "STOP!"

I share my story for those who did not have a safe adult to process with-for those who did not have someone to assure you, "What happened to you was not right! This was not your fault. There's nothing wrong with you! You're gonna be okay, my love. The people who hurt you were abusers and you did not deserve this! I'm so sorry for the people who should have loved you and comforted you, yet only cared about the way things looked. I'm so sorry for those who denied that these wrongs ever happened to you."

Yet even in the aftermath of such pain, there is a plan and a path forward.

Friend, with all my heart I want to tell you: *don't give up.* Wholeness is not a one-time event—it's a journey of continually seeking God, trusting Him, and letting Him into every place in your heart. He will answer. He will show up. He is faithful. I know the waiting can feel long, and I know how tempting it is to want instant results—but real restoration is too precious to rush. You've come too far to quit now. Keep going. You are worth the time, the fight, the tears, and the long-suffering it might take to be free.

Along the way, find a safe, trusted, Godly community to encourage and support you. Set firm boundaries with those who lack compassion or the heart of God. Guard your healing like the treasure it is. May the Lord Himself lead you into the very place you need to be for wholeness. May He repay you with divine recompense for your pain and loss.

The same God who unlocked the cage of a little girl's heart is now inviting me—and is inviting you—to partner with Him in unlocking cages all around us. Your story carries power. Your freedom can open prison doors for someone else. Stay the course. The Author of YOUR story is not finished yet!

* * *

Beyond becoming whole, pioneering a ministry, stepping into marriage, moving across the country, and reconciling with God and myself, my journey has been about breaking cycles. For years, I operated from a place where I was running away from cycles, rather than abolishing them. My overactive sense of responsibility was fueled by pain from childhood that I wanted to escape. My independence was charged by former abandonment. I've had to learn to not just react against generational patterns but to discontinue their impact completely, to cancel the assignment and uproot what the enemy had planted.

There's a Hebrew saying: "The actions of the fathers are assigned to the children." What one generation fails to confront often falls into the lap of the next. As I have grown in obedience and faith in God, I have seen destructive cycles broken in my own family. I also believe we are called to break cycles at a broader scale in society. I see new opportunities opening in media, film, government, and education. I want to move at the pace of grace as God expands the tent pegs of my life.

We are not called to survive the end times—we are called to shape them. Too many believers are waiting for rescue instead of advancing in purpose. Even in exile, God told His people to build, plant, multiply, and seek the welfare of their city. He said, "Do not shrink back!" (See Jeremiah 29:7.)

The same is true for us.

The Church must stop outsourcing responsibility to governments and step back into her original role: caring for the vulnerable, healing the sick, solving problems, and engaging culture with both truth and love. We must refuse the "us vs. them" mindset—that spirit is rooted in pride, not Christ. Real impact happens through humility, not hostility. It's time to pick up our sword and our trowel again—to build, to pray, to love, and to lead.

The enemy knows the power of unity. That's why he keeps the church distracted and divided. But if we could lay down our pride and truly come together—across denominations, across generations, across cultures—we would become unstoppable. What God is building now will require all of us: apostles, prophets, pastors, teachers, evangelists, intercessors, reformers, artists, and warriors. It will require both a soft heart and a strong hand. It will require both courage and compassion.

As for me and my household, we will keep saying *yes*.

It was in the little church under Pastor Bradshaw that I first learned what it meant to be faithful with little, to serve quietly, to worship freely, and to love people deeply. It taught me that greatness in the Kingdom doesn't come through platform—but through obedience. From those humble streets of South Gate to the stages and seasons God now has for me and Jarrett, His faithfulness has remained.

Every lesson, every wound, every healing, every encounter has led us to where we are today. The world is shaking, the Church is rising. In times like these, with the stories we have, we can choose to hide or to build. The need is clear, our time is short. By the grace of God, may we be found *building*.

Grandfather William McGuire and Elvis Presley

Justin and Sandi in South Gate, Ca

Lyn-Gate Neighborhood Church

Left to right: Sandi, Justin, Rachel with Phillip in her lap, and Margie

The Shift Gala, Washington, D.C.

Dr. Rachel Jones and Sandi

Jarrett and Sandi Ellis were married a second time by Dr. Corral in CA

Jarrett and Sandi Ellis were married first in Atlanta

Wedding in Atlanta, married by Alveda, Jarrett's Mom. She had just announced us as husband and wife, thus the triumphant look on her face.

Dr. Corral Wedding on Rosh Hashanah for CA family

Acknowledgements

Jarrett Ellis

You have been the steady strength that carried me across the finish line of this book. Long overdue, yes—but made possible by your unwavering support. Thank you for putting Jesus first and for loving me as Christ loves the Church. Thank you for giving me a voice, reaching for me in the hardest moments, and never letting go. Out of nearly 9 billion souls, the Creator of the universe chose you for me. That is nothing short of a miracle. I love you with all my heart. After Jesus, you are the sweetest treasure of my life.

Dr. Michelle Corral

Pastor, thank you for being a living signpost that points to Jesus in every way, shape, and form. Thank you for embodying the standard of a life fully surrendered to Christ. Your lamp is always filled with oil, burning brightly, so that those of us who are learning, watching, and gleaning from your example may also keep our lamps full.

Thank you for living the Gospel—on five fingers, every hour of every day—so that we might not only hear the

Word, but see it lived before our very eyes. Your life is a testimony, and I am forever grateful. Thank you for being a safe place for Jarrett and me. It means the world.

Pastor Paul and Kathy Bradshaw

There are no words for what you have surrendered so that thousands might be saved, healed, and delivered. Only God truly knows. "Thank you" feels far too small. I cry as I write this, knowing you have poured out your hearts, your lives, and all that you are into the ministry of Christ. I survived a rough beginning because of your obedience to the Lord, and I speak for many when I say—there is no earthly way to ever repay you...that one is on God.

Pastors Jerry and Kimberly Dirmann

Thank you for giving your life fully to Jesus in all you do. I have gleaned from your field many times, and I would not be here today without your help in building a solid life. Thank you for teaching us the vital importance of supporting Israel and standing firm on God's Word, no matter how things appear. On life's journey, God sent me to the best of the best, and I am forever grateful He did.

SANDI ELLIS is the Founder and President of Here Comes Joy Ministries and an ordained Prophet and Teacher. She is a sought-after apostolic voice, known for partnering with the Holy Spirit to bring about healing and spiritual breakthroughs. Through her ministry, she equips believers for their divine assignments, with joy as the natural outflow of liberty in Christ.

With a background in Biblical Hermeneutics from Melodyland School of Theology, Sandi ministers itinerantly and hosts the Here Comes Joy television program and podcast, featured on multiple networks. She also contributes regularly to prominent platforms, including CTN, American Family Radio, GoodVue, and the Vision Television Network. Additionally, her prophetic words have been published in The Elijah List and Spirit Fuel, expanding her reach to a global audience.

Having overcome profound trauma and hardship, Sandi now ministers healing—body, mind, and spirit—bringing hope and restoration to individuals and communities across the nation. Her testimony embodies the power of God's redeeming love and the joy that springs from a life made whole in Christ. She is married to Jarrett, a prominent attorney and minister, and together they live in the greater Atlanta area, traveling widely as they minister healing to the body of Christ.

www.ingramcontent.com/pod-product-compliance
Lightning Source LLC
Chambersburg PA
CBHW032151080426
42735CB00008B/660